BEFORE BILLY THE KID

The Boy behind the Legendary Outlaw

MELODY GROVES

TWODOT®

ESSEX, CONNECTICUT
HELENA, MONTANA

A TWO DOT BOOK
An imprint of Globe Pequot, the trade division of The Rowman & Littlefield
Publishing Group, Inc.
4501 Forbes Blvd., Ste. 200
Lanham, MD 20706
www.rowman.com

Distributed by NATIONAL BOOK NETWORK

British Library Cataloguing in Publication Information available

Library of Congress Cataloging-in-Publication Data

Names: Groves, Melody, 1952- author.
Title: Before Billy the Kid : the boy behind the legendary outlaw / Melody
  Groves.
Description: Guilford, Connecticut : TwoDot, [2022] | Includes
  bibliographical references and index. | Summary: "In Before Billy the
  Kid, author Melody Groves explores the early life of the infamous
  outlaw, the teenage boy who loved to sing and dance. The young man who
  was polite, educated, and popular. A boy who had the bad luck to be
  orphaned at fifteen and left with no one to guide him through life. How
  different history might have been if Billy had pursued his love of music
  instead of a life of crime" —Provided by publisher.
Identifiers: LCCN 2022004034 (print) | LCCN 2022004035 (ebook) | ISBN
  9781493063499 (paperback) | ISBN 9781493063505 (epub)
Subjects: LCSH: Billy, the Kid. | Outlaws—Southwest, New—Biography. | Southwest,
  New—Biography. | Billy, the Kid—Family.
Classification: LCC F786.B54 G76 2022 (print) | LCC F786.B54 (ebook) |
  DDC 364.1/552092 [B]—dc23/eng/20220203
LC record available at https://lccn.loc.gov/2022004034
LC ebook record available at https://lccn.loc.gov/2022004035

CONTENTS

ACKNOWLEDGMENTS

SOMETIMES A MERE "THANK YOU" IS NOT ENOUGH TO ACKNOWLedge the help someone has given in such a daunting undertaking as writing about Billy the Kid. But a big thanks and my heartfelt appreciation will have to suffice. My cowboy hat is off to the following:

Bob Boze Bell for graciously and generously allowing use of his work.

Ralph Estes for his work on Billy and his awesome book, *The Autobiography of Billy the Kid*.

Drew Gomber and **Scott Smith** for information and inspiration.

Kathy Wagoner, Phil Jackson, Judy Avila, Dennis Kastendiek, and **Don Morgan** for their amazing editorial and critiquing skills.

Silver City History Museum for being so accommodating and helpful in providing photos.

Wichita-Sedgewick Historical Society for easily and quickly allowing use of one of their treasure troves of photos.

Tara Woodruff for sharing such an amazing photo of her great-great grandfather.

Candy Moulton for her information about western trails.

Patti Hersey for allowing use of her husband's map.

Don Bullis and **Johnny Boggs** for their wide-ranging knowledge of western facts and always being willing to share not only their wisdom but also their notions about Billy.

Myke Groves for his support, wonderful photos, and "driving the bus."

AUTHOR'S NOTE: WHY BILLY?

*"He weighed about 125 pounds and was five feet seven inches
tall, and as straight as an arrow. The Kid had beautiful hazel
eyes. Those eyes so quick and piercing were what saved his life
many a time."*

—FRANK COE, BILLY'S FRIEND

July 14
Fort Sumner, New Mexico

TO THE SOUTH, AN OMINOUS WALL OF PURPLE-BLACK RAIN
clouds rolls across the sky, smothering a serene, cerulean blue.
Wind spurts, bringing ozone smells of rain and, with it, possible
hail. Pete Maxwell's hacienda, perched near the Pecos River, is
built of strong lumber and, it is hoped, will repel the storm's attack.

Billy the Kid has taken refuge at his friend's house. Naked
except for long johns and hungry for a snack, Billy rises from
Paulita Maxwell's bed. He promises her, rounded with child, to
bring back a slice of ham to help quell her upset stomach. He pulls
on trousers and makes his way barefoot across the *sala* toward the
back porch, where the ham hangs. Nerves tingle as he passes Pete's
bedroom. Something is off, doesn't feel right. While he knows he's
the number one most wanted man in the Southwest right now,
he knows also that Sheriff Pat Garrett is miles away on official
county business. At least that is what he has been told.

Reaching the porch, he finds a carving knife and picks it up. The hairs on his arms stand at attention again, his breaths come in short spurts. Something is undeniably wrong.

Maybe his friend Pete, Paulita's brother, would know something. Before slicing off a piece of ham, he backtracks to Pete's bedroom. The room is dark, but he senses someone sitting on the bed, hidden mostly by the open door.

"¿Quién es?" he asks. "Who is it?" he asks again in English.

In answer, orange sparks flash across the room. Burning fire pierces Billy's chest, directly above his heart. Another flash takes him to the floor, where his blood soaks into the wooden planks.

From here, the legend begins.

THIS IS WHERE IT BECOMES PERSONAL

This is not 1881, and this is not the actual killing of soft-spoken William Henry McCarty Antrim, alias Billy the Kid. Rather, it is 2006, and this is a reenactment of Billy's death. The New Mexico Gunfighters Association, a group founded in 1978 and known for their "Wild West" skits in Albuquerque's Old Town, has been invited as entertainment for Fort Sumner's annual Billy the Kid Days. They asked us to give visitors a true sense of what took place. And we obliged.

Fort Sumner, Gathering Spot for the Area

Named after former New Mexico Territory military governor Edwin Vose Sumner, the fort was charged with the internment of the territory's Navajo and Mescalero Apache populations from 1863 to 1868. With the fort's closing, the government sold its buildings to Lucien Maxwell.

Lucien B. Maxwell irrigated the land, raised crops, and ran a herd of cattle on it until his death in 1875. Lucien's widow, Luz, retained ownership of the buildings. The Maxwell family entered into an agreement with Emanuel Brazil, a local rancher, and formed the Brazil and Maxwell Horseshoe Ranch. Cattle management fell to Pete Maxwell. Since the ranch controlled the water over most of this part of the country, it became the largest agricultural operation in the area.

The buildings were sold in 1884 to the New England Cattle Company. A 1935 Works Progress Association report stated that the old fort was torn down for the lumber that it contained. The heavier timbers, doors, windows, and other lumber were carried away and used in other buildings. Charlie Foor, an old-time resident, helped tear down the old Maxwell home and used the flooring in his present home.

In the 1920s, the Transcontinental Air Transport airline built an airfield in Fort Sumner as part of its coast-to-coast air passenger network, but the site was abandoned when the airline's ambitious plans collapsed in the Great Depression. The airfield was reopened by the U.S. Air Force as a training base during World War II. After the war, the base became the Fort Sumner Municipal Airport and was chosen as a launch site for NASA's high-altitude balloon program.

Today, Fort Sumner is a ranching village boasting more than 1,000 residents along with at least two fascinating Billy the Kid museums.

By this point, I'd been a member of the Gunfighters for many years and had traveled and performed all over New Mexico. But this reenactment was truly awe inspiring, memorable, and absolutely chilling. The town of Fort Sumner had put up painted plywood backdrops of Maxwell's bedroom and outer rooms on the house's original site. We stood where Maxwell's hacienda used to stand (the foundation was washed away in a 1937 Pecos River flood). That house was the original Fort Sumner built in 1860 to quarter U.S. Army officers during the forced relocations of the Mescalero Apache and Navajo.

The Gunfighters actors faced north. I was lucky enough to be narrator, so I faced south, watching the show over the heads of more than 100 seated spectators.

We started our performance with Billy telling Paulita he'd be right back, while in the southern sky, boiling violet clouds rolled in. The other actors couldn't see the approaching storm, but I sure could. And then the most amazing, scary, and best-timed event *ever* happened.

Just as Sheriff Pat Garrett pulled the gun and shot, not only did orange flash across the room (we use black powder and blanks—the actors' safety being paramount), but lightning zig-zagged across the sky, sprinting from one side to the other. The angry clouds turned silver, and wind kicked up dust, carrying that ozone smell that attacked my senses. I gasped, as did many of the audience members. I couldn't breathe. It was *so* real.

They loaded Billy onto a horse-drawn wagon and led him south. A line of mourners, actors, and audience members flanked the wagon and plodded straight into that storm. Many spectators wept.

For me, a truly enchanting, memorable moment.

As a side note, after much persuasion, the actor who portrayed Billy quite reluctantly agreed to shave off his mustache, one he'd groomed since high school. The next day, he started growing it again. Jeff definitely sacrificed for his art.

SO CLOSE TO HISTORY
Another New Mexico Gunfighters event took us to Puerto de Luna (which the explorer Francisco Coronado dubbed the "Gateway of the Moon"), a lovely tiny village ten miles southeast of Santa Rosa, New Mexico, in the middle of Billy the Kid territory.

As chance would have it, we performed for a bikers' rally on the grounds of the historic 1874 Alexander Grzelachowski mercantile store in Puerto de Luna.

Now on the National Register of Historic Places, Alexander Grzelachowski's Puerto de Luna Mercantile is where Billy the Kid ate his last Christmas supper.

PHOTO COURTESY OF JAMES BLACKBURN, NEW MEXICO GUNFIGHTERS ASSOCIATION

Polish-born Grzelachowski is best remembered by historians as the Puerto de Luna merchant who served Billy the Kid his last Christmas dinner on December 25, 1880, when Sheriff Pat Garrett transported the fugitive to Las Vegas, where he would take the train south to La Mesilla to stand trial.

The first time I stepped into the Grzelachowski building, the eighteen-inch adobe walls breathed out cool air in the middle of a hot summer. Listed on the state historical registry, the mercantile building also breathed history, complete with well-worn threshold strips and wooden floors, one section in the back of the store soaked with old blood. A large-caliber bullet hole in the wall tells the story. Locals denied a shooting, instead cited "chicken plucking," but the evidence was clear.

If that wasn't fascinating enough, sitting under the shade of the portico was an old man. No offense to the "older generation," but this man was *old*. Had to be pushing ninety-five if a day. I couldn't help but spend time chatting with him. He told me that his father remembered going to the *bailes* (dances) where Billy Bonney two-stepped the night away with señoritas not only from Puerto de Luna (PDL as locals call it) but from the surrounding ranches as well.

The older gentleman reported that his father thought Billy a fine dancer and a most pleasant individual. And the girls loved him.

So much for six degrees of separation! How about one?

I kick myself for not getting the exact spelling of the man's name and his age. I've returned to PDL a few times since then and have yet to meet him again. However, *once* I had the opportunity to speak to living history, and for that I'm ever grateful.

BILLY THE KID IS MY OUTLAW

In many ways, Billy the Kid is *my* outlaw and my hero. I grew up in Las Cruces, southern New Mexico, next to the village of La Mesilla, where, in early 1881, Billy Bonney was brought to stand trial for shooting and killing Sheriff William Brady. The fact that there were six other Regulators shooting at Brady did not mean much to Sheriff Pat Garrett and Governor Lew Wallace. They needed a scapegoat, and Billy was handy. In fact, he was the only man ever tried for that murder. He spent a few weeks in a jail that faced La Mesilla plaza.

My house sat in a century-old pecan orchard about a mile from La Mesilla. Growing up, a neighbor kid and I would often wander through cotton fields and past an old abandoned adobe house to end up in La Mesilla. I'd walk the plaza's cobble streets and duck into the original jail, which today is a souvenir shop. My young mind watched Billy in front of a jury, pleading his case but to no avail. I even envisioned him escaping through a narrow side window and loping down an alley, jumping on a horse and galloping to freedom. Of course, factually, that never happened *there*. It did, however, take place in the town of Lincoln, where he escaped to Fort Sumner. And we know how *that* ended.

But still, I've always considered him mine.

And now, after mountains of research, I'm able to put things into perspective. He was a man of his time, a boy who did the best he could under trying circumstances, a boy forced into adulthood before he was ready. His physical appearance betrayed him. Young looking, slight of build, and with slim hands and a soft voice, he was often mistaken for a young teen. He was a boy/man who desperately needed to be taken seriously. The only way he knew how was by the gun.

I now understand him and want to share his story.

Yep. Billy the Kid is definitely *my* outlaw.

INTRODUCTION:
WHO WAS BILLY THE KID, REALLY?

"What was left was the lone figure, all at once romantic and daring but also dark and lethal. He had become both outlaw myth and mythical hero."

—MICHAEL WALLIS, AUTHOR OF
BILLY THE KID: THE ENDLESS RIDE

"I THINK OF THE MORN WHEN I SAILED AWAY FROM THEE. I SAID pray to God for me, pray to God for me." Billy McCarty sang along to "La Paloma"[1] and twirled his mother around the wooden dance floor. "I longed once more for Mother's sweet face." Twelve-year-old Billy squeezed Catherine's hand gently but firmly. Words to this two-step jig, in Spanish and English, flowed together in the southwestern town of Silver City.

The music, courtesy of a squeeze box, fiddle, and guitar, crescendoed, then ended. Billy bowed to his mom, and she curtsied to him, smiles brightening both faces. His mother beamed. She and Billy often sang and danced together, making quite the couple. The crowd clapped enthusiastically while her eyes sparkled, and Billy fought to catch his breath.

The band struck up again. This time, beats of "Patrick's Day Parade"[2] got Billy's feet tapping. He and Catherine once again took the dance floor, twirling from one end of the room to the other. Dancers tried to keep up, but Billy and his mom outdanced everyone.

Directly influenced by his mother, Billy loved to sing and dance, attending *bailes* in the general store in Puerto de Luna and in saloons and houses in Santa Rosa, Fort Sumner, Anton Chico (New Mexico), Tascosa (Texas), and anywhere there was a fiddle and a girl. He'd escort pretty señoritas onto the dance floor and "make merry" long into the night. Who could not love such a man who embraced life?

Could this be the same teenager who a few years later would be accused of carving twenty-one notches on his gun? The low-life scoundrel who killed at random? The bilingual man who couldn't be trusted around women? A man with no moral compass? The worst of the worst? Could this be the same man?

Billy the Kid wasn't "Billy the Kid" until the *Las Vegas Gazette* labeled him with that nickname in late 1880. He was born William Henry McCarty. Billy acquired the label of "the Kid" as a young teenager, when he first associated with grown men. His boyish face and slim figure belied the maturity he held inside. "More than any other trait, youth shaped the personality and directed the life of Billy the Kid."[3] He would later go by Henry McCarty, Billy Antrim, Henry Antrim, Kid Antrim, the Kid, William H. Bonney, Billy Bonney, Billito, and El Chivato. Regardless of the moniker, he's the same person.

And was he really that bad? History is full of myths, half-truths, and conjecture. Truth is, we'll never know for sure exactly how many men Billy the Kid killed: two or twenty-two? We'll never know what he would have done if life hadn't been so unkind to him. He simply couldn't catch a break.

That's not to say everyone else in the 1860s had it easy. Many immigrants, such as his mother, Catherine McCarty, who immigrated from Ireland, had a rough time entering America and making a go of it. Met with prejudice, lack of employment opportunities, and a new country, many failed, pinning their hopes on the next generation to have an easier life. No doubt, Billy's mother thought the same way. But what set her son apart? What made him a celebrity of the notorious kind? Was he really all that evil? That fast with a gun? Did he deserve all the press? And what about the pardon by Governor Lew Wallace that was promised but denied?

Life was hardscrabble. Society of that day, in pre–Civil War times and beyond, lacked the safety nets we enjoy today. There was no Social Security, no sort of retirement afforded the working class. Certainly, there were churches to help and a few aid societies, such as widows and orphans societies, but they could do only so much. Friends relied on each other for help, but again, that went only so far. Family helped family. But in Billy McCarty's case, there was no family. After age thirteen, he had an unknown biological father, an absent stepfather, a deceased mother, an estranged brother, and no other recognized relatives.

"And like any other myth, Billy the Kid is a chameleon who changes appearance with each succeeding story. We have lost the authentic Billy, the boy who grew up on a harsh frontier in which many people found his actions more ennobling than criminal."[4] No one thought to ask his childhood friends, when they were still relatively young, what they truly remembered. "Mythmaking thrives where fact is scarce, and, as a result, only a skeletal reconstruction of the boyhood of Billy the Kid is possible."[5]

"Sometimes regarded as a Robin Hood stealing from the rich to help the poor, as a lone individual holding out against the corrupt Santa Fe Ring, Billy was inducted early on into the pantheon of Wild West heroes . . . the Kid has exploded into a gigantic mythic figure."[6]

Peeling off layers of legends accumulated over a century of purple prose and writers unafraid to embellish the truth "a bit," a complex individual lies exposed. Billy McCarty would have been lost to history had it not been for fateful decisions made either *by* him or *for* him. Billy did not get a fair shake in life.

Billy the Kid was cobbled together by injustices and bad decisions.

Yet there is another aspect of that young man often overlooked. His human side.

CHAPTER ONE

AND SO, IT BEGINS

"Through the years many historians and writers have lost sight of the fact that the Kid was just that: a kid."
—MICHAEL WALLIS, AUTHOR OF
BILLY THE KID: THE ENDLESS RIDE

LIKE MANY CHILDREN OF THE NINETEENTH CENTURY, BILLY'S beginnings are shrouded in mystery. It isn't clear exactly where or when William Henry McCarty was born.

"Later on I told people a lot of different ages," Billy stated to a reporter when asked about his age. "Mostly because I wanted them to think I was old enough to be taken seriously. [Sheriff Pat] Garrett and [writer Ash] Upson wrote that I was born in 1859—and they gave me the same birthday as Upson, November 23. I think I was actually born a little later than that, maybe '61 or '62, but what does it matter?"[1]

It matters quite a bit. Maybe not to him, but it does to myriad historians and Billy aficionados who want to understand this American icon. Generally, historians have believed he was born in 1859. That date is most likely wrong due to Ash Upson, who wrote a great deal of Sheriff Pat Garrett's book, *The Authentic Life of Billy the Kid*. Upson attributed his own birthday of November 23 to Billy and randomly picked 1859 as his birth year.

I

New research points to Billy being born in May 1861. If he was indeed born then, that would explain why he looked so young as an outlaw. Many accounts spoke of peach fuzz on the upper lip when he was supposedly eighteen, and so many friends said he looked younger than he was reported to be. Did Billy truly know his birth date? Doesn't sound like it. As was customary, births, marriages, and deaths were all recorded in a family Bible, passed down through the generations. Unfortunately, no such McCarty family Bible has ever been found.

"Historians cannot agree on the place and date of the Kid's birth, simply because no one has found any compelling evidence for the claims. The Billy the Kid Outlaw Gang organization is offering $500 'to the first person who finds irrefutable proof of Henry McCarty's birth, his father, and where he was born.' No one has yet claimed the reward."[2]

So, for sake of argument, we'll stick with May 1861 as the year of his birth, although we may never know for certain.

Despite the question of his birth date, what is not in doubt is his name: William Henry McCarty. In 1873, he listed himself as a witness to his mother's wedding (to Bill Antrim), written as "William H. McCarty."

WHAT ABOUT DAD AND MOM?

Many reputable historians have plowed through legal documents, historical archives, period newspapers, marriage certificates, baptismal records, census records, city directories, and every other available source to find the factual history of Billy. Their efforts have been met with irritatingly little success.

William's McCarty father is unknown. Speculation has run rampant. Historians, researchers, and biographers each have their own theories about Mr. McCarty—if that was his name.

The closest nugget of information comes from Billy's mom, Catherine McCarty (possibly née Devine), who told compilers of the Indianapolis City Directory that she was the widow of

Michael McCarty. She provided no further details. With not much else to go on, historians generally agree that the information is correct, and Billy's probable father was Michael. Researchers have been unable to lock down *which* Michael.

We do know for certain his mother was Catherine McCarty, most likely an Irish refugee. One passenger list of the *Devonshire* reveals a Catherine McCarty departing Liverpool, then arriving in New York on April 10, 1846. Catherine, born in 1829 or 1830 (which are seemingly reliable dates since her 1874 obituary listed her as forty-five), would have been sixteen when she arrived on American soil. Her occupation on the ship's passenger roster was listed as "servant," which more than likely meant that she was indentured to a wealthy family. Her term of contract would have been for the customary seven years. Many immigrants settled in and around New York City.

Irish Immigration in the Nineteenth Century

Leaving Ireland as one of the thousands of "Famine Irish," Catherine McCarty would have set sail for America by first taking a ferry or a boat from Cobh, Dublin, or Belfast, Ireland, and would have disembarked in Liverpool, England. There passengers would have transferred to a larger ship bound for Canada, Boston, New York, or New Orleans. During the horrific Potato Famine (1845–1854), tens of thousands of men, women, and children left their homeland in search of a better life.

"The combination of famine and disease and the resulting immigration reduced Ireland's population from 8.1 million in 1840 to 6.5 million a decade later."[3] Even today, in the twenty-first century, the population has not recovered.

Prior to 1855, immigrants would have sailed into the docks on the east side of Manhattan, where little to no processing took place.

Passengers arriving in 1855 and later would have been processed at Emigrant Landing Depot, known as Castle Garden, New York. As America's first official immigrant receiving center, Castle Garden opened that year, welcoming more than 8 million refugees before closing on April 18, 1890. To replace the center, a large warehouse was used for two years until Ellis Island opened in 1892.

AND WHAT ABOUT BILLY?

There is little consensus as to where exactly Billy, who went by the name Henry as a youngster, was born. Various researchers list Ireland, New York, Indianapolis, Missouri, Illinois, and New Mexico as definitive places of birth. One of those is probably correct.

Unfortunately, Billy's status as a wanted man often required friends to lie for him, so even government records can't always be trusted. For example, in 1880 at Fort Sumner, New Mexico, Manuela Bowdre, the wife of Billy's good friend Charlie, told a federal census taker that Billy was William Henry McCarty, that he was twenty-five years old, that both his parents had been born in Missouri, and that he, too, had been born there. By the time the census in 1880 came around, Billy was a fugitive with a $500 bounty on his head, often found hanging out at the Bowdre ranch. Most people knew him as Billy Bonney, so by telling the census worker that he was William Henry McCarty, born in Missouri and age twenty-five, Manuela might have figured she was protecting her friend.

There are no records indicating that either of Billy's parents were born in Missouri. His mother spoke with a lovely Irish lilt, commented on often by her friends. Chances are good she was born and raised in Ireland.

Of all the possible birthplaces that have been tossed around for 100 years, two remain probable: New York City and Indianapolis.

If purple-prose writers of the wild-and-woolly western tales had their way, Billy was born in New York. According to journalists in the 1870s and 1880s who played loose with facts (anything to sell a newspaper), New York City would be the perfect place to cite as the Kid's birthplace. Tall tales detailing the exploits of one of their own would certainly sell mountains of dime novels, magazines, and newspapers on the East Coast, where people were fascinated by the Wild West and western desperados. So why not portray this desperado as a New Yorker who headed west? No one would question the accuracy.

However, recent research is pointing more to his birthplace as Utica, New York. Catherine worked for a wealthy family in that city. Some argue, logically, that William Henry McCarty was likely born in Indiana, possibly Indianapolis, because Catherine McCarty showed up in the Indianapolis City Directory in 1868 with the home address of 199 North East Street. Neither of her sons was listed, which, unfortunately, was a common practice.

But why would Catherine travel all the way west to Indiana? Relocating two young sons from New York City or Utica to Indianapolis on her own would be a challenge even under good circumstances. She had to have had a compelling reason to move.

Indianapolis had become a hub of the Midwest in the 1860s, full of army forts. Maybe she relocated to Indiana because the 35th Indiana Infantry Regiment, the state's first Irish American regiment, was organized at Indianapolis in 1861. Perhaps her husband Michael McCarty enlisted in the Union army there.

Indiana was also home to Camp Morton, a major prisoner-of-war camp for Confederate prisoners in 1862. Although there is no logical reason a man from New York would join the Confederate cause, it is possible Catherine's husband was a Confederate soldier, captured and then imprisoned in Indianapolis. But, logically, would a young woman with two small children travel all the way from New York to Indiana to be close to her imprisoned husband? Not likely. No, she would stay home, as did thousands of other wives, and hope and pray he'd make it back alive.

During the war years, Indianapolis's population escalated, and businesses sprung up, offering ample employment opportunities. Did Catherine see the opportunity of opening her own business—a laundry and boardinghouse?

With the booming population came a wide variety of entertainment. Theaters and performances of all types captivated crowds. These attractions included minstrel shows, burlesque, variety shows, circuses, operettas, concerts, drama, opera, and others. For thirty-something Catherine McCarty, a spry Irish woman who loved to sing and dance, this must have been a wonderful place to live.

WHAT ABOUT CATHERINE'S OTHER SON, JOSEPH?

Billy wasn't Catherine's only son. Around 1863, she gave birth to Joseph Bonney McCarty, possibly in Utica, New York. Of course, questions linger about the identity of Joseph's father but also of Joseph's year of birth.

Many records point to 1863. Joseph gave his age as seventeen in the 1880 Colorado census, meaning he would have been born in 1863—making him two years *younger* than Billy. Backed by convincing evidence is an 1885 Arapahoe County, Colorado, census showing his age as twenty-one, again making him born in 1863. And then on a voting registration form that Joseph filled out in October 1916, he gave his age as fifty-three, making his birth year 1863.

There is little doubt he was born in 1863, two years *after* his brother Billy.

Questions have surrounded Billy and Joseph's relationship for years. Did they get along? More than likely they did, although there is no record of Josie (as he was called) attending any of the dances his mom and brother enjoyed.

Billy and his brother grew up together moving from possibly New York to Indiana to Kansas to Denver to New Mexico, first Santa Fe and then Silver City. Were they close siblings? Certainly, they went to school together, being two of thirty students, and did chores together, but not much has been written about Billy's brother.

The boys' lives in Silver City have been well documented through memoirs of their childhood friends, school records, and newspaper accounts. They were, in all probability, half brothers, especially when comparing appearances. Billy was described as small for his age with slender and delicate hands, small feet, and a soft, high voice. His Silver City friend, Anthony Conner, figured "he was undersized, and really girlish looking. I don't think he weighed over seventy-five pounds." However, no doubt in Anthony's mind, in 1873, "Billy was about twelve years old." Best known for his famous slightly bucked front teeth, Billy smiled and laughed often. Friend Chauncey Truesdell remembered Billy as "a mild mannered, flaxen-haired, blue-eyed boy."[4]

Joseph, however, was "larger and very husky," said Chauncey. "He looked to be a year and a half or two older than Henry."[5]

WHERE DID THE NAME "BONNEY" COME FROM?

Theories run rampant about Joseph's middle name and the Kid's use of the name Bonney (i.e., William H. Bonney, Billy Bonney). Where did it come from?

One theory that makes sense about the name Bonney suggests that while living in Utica, New York, lovely early thirty-something Catherine worked for John Munn and his wealthy family. In the 1860 census, we find that (according to the 1858–1859 city directory) eight doors up the street lived John J. Bonney and Edward Finch Bonney, one older and one younger than Catherine.[6]

Rumors flew of a tryst or liaison, but with which brother is unclear. Was Joseph's father a Bonney? Otherwise, why did she choose to give her son the middle name of Bonney? And why did

Billy choose that particular surname as an alias? Coincidence? Probably not.

Another conjecture is that Bonney is Catherine's actual maiden name. Some historians theorize it could be her first married name, with McCarty and Antrim coming later. Other historians think Billy was calling himself "handsome" since *bonney/ bonnie* in Irish means "good looking." *Bonito* in Spanish means "pretty." (The valley in which Lincoln sits is Bonito Valley.) Was he calling himself "Billy the Beautiful?" He *was* known for his sense of humor. Will we ever know for sure? Probably not.

A LOGICAL DEDUCTION

Two big questions have been presented here. Why did Catherine move from New York to Indianapolis, a journey of more than 700 miles, with two small children, and where did the Bonney name come from? These produce more questions.

This author has put together reasonings that make sense. While certain facts are concrete, some are conjecture, but human nature hasn't changed in the past several hundred years. It was 1868 when we know Catherine was in Indianapolis. If Billy was born in 1861, he would have been around seven and Joseph probably around five.

More than likely, a year or two after Michael McCarty died, Catherine fell in love with one of the Bonney men, either John or Edward. Their liaison produced a son, Joseph Bonney McCarty. Catherine was a blue-collar working-class woman, most likely Catholic, *and* pregnant outside of marriage. Living in a mainly Protestant, anti-Irish environment, no doubt when Bonney's well-to-do family discovered Catherine was with child, the family erupted with disdain. Probably being concerned about their standing in society (after all, how would it look to other well-financed families of New York?), they considered options. With the knowledge their son produced an illegitimate heir to their kingdom, they did one of two things: the Bonney family disinherited their son (which would certainly cause a scandal) or, most likely, made Catherine leave. Otherwise, why else would she travel so far?

In all likelihood, Bonney escorted Catherine and the two boys to Indianapolis—possibly as far west as the train traveled. Assuming he still had access to family money, he set her up in Indiana with a house and possibly tools to run a business. If he was truly invested, Bonney probably sent her money from time to time, like a modern-day child support payment. From there, they went their separate ways.

In Indianapolis, she identified herself as Michael McCarty's widow in the 1868 census because she *was*. Society of the day would have shunned a woman who admitted to having one (or both) of her children born out of wedlock and divorced women too. It was much easier to admit being a widow, something quite common after the Civil War.

CHAPTER TWO

LITTLE HOUSE ON THE FRONTIER

"He was a mere boy in appearance, always jovial and high-spirited; but in an emergency he always stood out as a leader, quick, resolute and firm."

—GEORGE L. BARBER
(SECOND HUSBAND OF SUSAN McSWEEN)

ENTER BILL ANTRIM

CIVIL WAR LIFE FOR CATHERINE IN INDIANAPOLIS MUST HAVE been difficult, especially with no husband to help guide two growing boys. In order to make ends meet and put food on the table, she baked goods and took in washing and boarders, something she would continue to do for the rest of her life.

Just how exactly Catherine McCarty met William Henry Harrison Antrim in Indianapolis is anybody's guess. Bill Antrim was a twenty-five-year-old laborer and teamster, one who drove wagons and lived a few blocks away. Had he delivered something to Catherine? Had she taken in his wash? No matter the circumstances, Catherine and Bill met around 1865, and thus began a long-term relationship.

More is known about the person who became Billy the Kid's stepfather, Bill Antrim, than is known about the McCarty clan.

Born at Huntsville, Indiana, in 1842 (this made him twelve years Catherine's junior), Bill was the fifth boy in a family of seven. Bill's father, Levi, was a merchant and proprietor of a hotel in nearby Anderson. While in school, Bill Antrim and his siblings washed dishes, hauled wood, and waited tables at the hotel.

In June 1862, twenty-year-old Bill Antrim enlisted in the Union army, mustering in as a private with the 54th Regiment of the Indiana Volunteer Infantry. He and the troops marched forty-two miles to Indianapolis, and then Antrim spent three months on guard duty at Camp Morton before he mustered out of service. From the few photographs available, he was about five feet, ten inches tall with a fair complexion, light-colored hair, and blue-gray eyes. He was slim but strongly built with somewhat stooped shoulders.

Staying in the city, he moved to 58 Cherry Street and became a driver and clerk at the Merchants Union Express Company, located within a few blocks from the McCarty residence on North East Street.

In the mid-1860s, Indianapolis was poised to house the steam locomotives bringing goods and people to and from the West. By this time, it boomed with commerce, using coal as power. Indianapolis choked with coal smoke filling the air, darkening skies, making eyes and noses water, and making breathing difficult. Little thought was given to what effects such particulates in the air would do to people's health. Progress was at hand, and nothing would stop commercial growth.

Was this where Catherine contracted tuberculosis, known then as consumption? Crowded city conditions and cold, wet weather, combined with her hands in hot, sudsy water all day, certainly may have contributed to her catching such a disease. Since laundry was her business, Catherine spent most of her days in a closed-off, steamy environment. Although her business was successful, she looked to move somewhere drier and less crowded in the hopes of improving her health.

WICHITA BOUND

Although Indianapolis offered many employment possibilities, the state had become settled, and much of the land was privately owned. Times were exciting, and new territories were opening for settlement. In 1869, the government offered the Osage Indian Trust Lands in Kansas to the general public for homestead settlement.[1] Requirements? Move onto a 160-acre quarter section of land and within five years perform certain improvements. Homesteading required minimal financing, which suited Catherine and Bill's situation. Catherine had to move to satisfy a craving to own property, and where better than a growing frontier town to raise her boys? Catherine's tuberculosis had to have been another driving factor. Doctors knew the only hope—no cure, just hope—was a dry climate. Wichita, Kansas, was drier. And clearer.

Wichita sounded perfect.

Whether it was for clearer skies or the excitement of moving to a growing frontier town, Catherine and her boys, nine-year-old Billy and seven-year-old Josie, shrugged off gray skies and cold, wet winters and headed west for Wichita in 1870.

Bill Antrim went too.

Aware of the stigma brought by the impropriety of two unmarried adults living together, upon arriving, Antrim bought property and built a cabin six miles outside of town. There he worked as a small farmer. Catherine resided in town. She and the boys lived upstairs in the building where she ran her laundry service on North Main Street.

It was here where William Henry McCarty would spend fourteen months on the real frontier, influenced by truly wild and unruly frontier characters.

Located in the heart of Wichita's up-and-coming business district, Catherine McCarty's City Laundry attracted a steady stream of customers from the day she opened. Her business did well enough to merit mention in the March 15, 1871, inaugural edition of the *Wichita Tribune*:

Wichita, Kansas, main street, ca. 1870. On July 21, 1870, Catherine McCarty signed a petition to incorporate the town of Wichita. Of 124 signers, she was the only woman. William Antrim signed below her. The judge granted the petition, and the town of Wichita was born.

PHOTO COURTESY OF WICHITA/SEDGWICK COUNTY HISTORICAL MUSEUM

The City Laundry is kept by Mrs. McCarty,
To whom we recommend those
Who wish to have their linen made clean[2]

Wichita's Humble Start

Near the end of the Civil War, Jesse Chisolm (not to be confused with cattle baron John Simpson Chisum), a Scot Cherokee trader and honorary member of the Wichita tribe, settled on the plains near a village of peaceful Wichita Indians. Here he established a trading post. In addition to the post, Chisolm, with the help of Black Beaver, a Lenape (Delaware) guide and rancher, plotted a path where cattle could be driven from Texas ranches to Kansas railheads. It remained as such until the Atchison, Topeka, and Santa Fe Railroad built a branch line in Wichita in 1872.

Newspapers of the 1870s abounded with tales of the crusty pioneer trailblazer, but they failed to mention that Chisolm had died in 1868 on the North Fork of the Canadian River in Indian Territory. Seems he'd eaten bear grease contaminated by a melted brass kettle.[3] How and why that happened is a mystery.

The Chisholm Trail became a crucial part of the American West's development in the late nineteenth century with 35,000 head of cattle traveling north the first year. Almost 5 million passed from Texas to Kansas in the following years. Alongside those cattle rode dusty, thirsty trail hands and cowboys.

Wichita blossomed into a rough-and-tumble place surrounded by an endless sea of grass that had long been the domain of Indians, buffalo hunters, and fur traders. Wichita vied with Abilene for the unofficial title of the wickedest city on the plains, complete with signs declaring, "Everything goes in Wichita."[4] A St. Louis paper described the town as a "brevet hell after sundown" with brass bands, piano music, and whip cracking in public streets contributing to the merriment. Reports of races between naked saloon girls kept the men in town.

Wichita struggled to keep its citizens safe and civil, thanks to numerous well-known lawmen who passed through, such as Wyatt Earp in 1874. Wichita had its share of quirks and questionable morals, while another town, Delano, sprung up across the bank of the Arkansas River. The rowdiness and debauchery, suppressed in Wichita, had to go somewhere, and Delano fit the bill. Delano became a village of saloons and brothels with a particular reputation for lawlessness. It accommodated the rough visiting cattlemen. Understandably, the Wichita/Delano community gained a wild reputation. Often, Delano's rowdiness spilled over into Wichita.

Generally, lawmen were few and far between, which meant citizens were responsible for meting out justice. Retribution for wrongdoing was swift, brutal, and often dispensed by persons other than law officers. A week or so before Billy and his family arrived, a vigilante posse had chased down a pair of horse thieves and immediately lynched them from a cottonwood limb (sometimes called a "jury limb").[5]

When Billy McCarty arrived, Wichita was a fledgling village with few amenities. Crude boardwalks flanked streets thick with mud or layers of dust. Water for drinking and cooking or for a special-occasion bath was hauled from springs, shallow wells, or cisterns. Most citizens lived in dugouts—a good idea during tornado season—or crude wooden cabins. Due to the scarcity of wood and the cost of coal, dried buffalo and cattle manure served as fuel. Cottonwood sprouts pulled from the riverbanks were planted to replace trees destroyed by prairie fires. Rattlesnakes and wolves were common. Winters were brutal, plunging to as low as -20°F, and summer temperatures were unbearable, reaching as high as 110°F.

Billy and Josie most likely didn't attend school because the only thing close to one was an abandoned army dugout that collapsed within the year. The village's first schoolmaster was hired for $45 a month and paid for his students' books out of his own pocket, having to order them from Topeka. At the close of the first term, he was in so much debt that he quit teaching and became a surveyor.

Apparently, Catherine took time to school her sons as both learned to read, write, and cipher. In fact, Billy became an avid reader.

CATHERINE: MOTHER AND BUSINESSWOMAN

Catherine was not your average woman of that era. Strong willed, independent, and spunky, she was a businesswoman who involved herself in town politics. Out of 124 town leaders asked to sign a petition for incorporation of the town, she was the *only woman.* She even attended the board of trustees meeting in McAdam's Hall. Wichita was incorporated as an official town on July 21, 1870.

Her City Laundry did a brisk trade thanks to the bundles of soiled doves' and brothel linens left at the door along with the piles of grimy clothing of the working class.[6] She scrubbed cowboys' mud-encrusted shirts and their silk neckerchiefs (also called wild rags) along with buffalo hunters' bloody pants and shirts. With Catherine busy washing, Bill Antrim worked as a part-time bartender and carpenter, using Billy's and Josie's help when possible.

Wichita's population boomed after incorporation. Within a couple of years, the new town boasted the third-largest population in all of Kansas. And the bad influences increased right along with it. What a delicious place to be as a young, impressionable boy. Easily influenced, Billy could take his pick from an assortment of soldiers, bullwhackers, sodbusters, renegades, Indians, wolf and buffalo hunters, misfits, scouts, and many of the rowdiest drovers ever to mount a horse. Catherine wanted better for her sons and hoped to avoid the tawdry influences of the men in town. Turns out that avoidance proved impossible.

A shootout between a former outlaw and a deputy U.S. marshal occurred just down the street from the City Laundry where the McCarty family lived. No doubt, Billy heard the gunfire or may have even witnessed the shooting. The outlaw died, and the marshal was wounded. Within four days, Catherine moved the boys and herself out of town and into Bill Antrim's cabin. Ignoring proper society for the moment, she wanted her sons safe.

As her laundry business prospered, Catherine began to dabble in real estate. Among many purchases, she bought a downtown vacant lot, while Antrim purchased a plot next to her laundry as well as the lot on which the business sat. He later deeded them over to Catherine.

In 1871, she filed claim on a quarter section out of town in Sedgwick County adjacent to Antrim's property. Antrim swore in a deposition that the McCarty family had moved out of the city and had been living on the claim since March 4. Antrim, with help from the boys, had built the family a cabin that was "12 by 14 feet, 1 story high, board roof, 1 door and 2 windows." The sale of the quarter section was approved, and Catherine paid $1.25 per acre, or a total of $200 cash, for her land.[7]

That summer, she and her sons cultivated seven acres and set out fifty-seven fruit trees. They enclosed a large plot of land with split rails and put in long rows of Osage orange trees. In late summer, Billy and Josie picked sand plums along the creek and riverbanks while Catherine and Bill enjoyed the pleasure of sweet elderberry wine. Life was certainly looking up for the blended family.

PERILS OF FRONTIER LIFE

Living on the open prairie in Wichita was dangerous. Texas long-horn cattle stampeded through property while being driven into the rail yard. Natural disasters like floods, twisters, and, worst of all, brush fires were a constant worry. Creepy critters such as rattle-snakes, scorpions, wolves, and coyotes prowled day and night. Also on the prowl at night were rough men, out-of-control liquored-up drovers, gunfighters with something to prove, and unscrupulous thieves, all now frequenting the town, causing trouble.

While Billy and his brother received little to no official "book learning," they certainly learned a lot from the streets. During the fourteen months they lived in Wichita, they watched buffalo hides being pegged out to dry, penetrating the air with the feral odor. Bits of putrid meat clinging to the shaggy skins and great piles of horse dung in the streets attracted enormous swarms of pesky bluebottle flies.

Being a conscientious mother, Catherine probably had second (maybe even third) thoughts on bringing up her sons in this hostile environment. Both impressionable sons may have started displaying actions like what they saw the cowboys do. And then life changed. Catherine realized her disease had returned. In those days, the only remedy for consumption sufferers was to live in a dry and warm climate. "A stifling hot laundry was far from the ideal place for someone battling consumption. Tubs of dirty clothing to be scrubbed with brushes and bars of strong yellow soap . . . linens boiling in soapy water with a tub of cold water nearby into which she could plunge her hands to prevent scalded flesh."[8] The warm and hot water creating a humid, closed-in environment, Catherine's tuberculosis took hold. Her health plummeted.

On the frontier, there were hardly any hospitals. Sick folks, even those afflicted with tuberculosis, had few options but to rest at home as much as possible. Those who could manage would leave, seeking a cure elsewhere rather than wasting away.

Catherine eagerly took her doctor's advice to relocate. She sold off her laundry business along with her real estate properties, and the family, including Bill, moved out West by the end of the summer of 1871. When Catherine decided to leave Wichita, Antrim purchased more land in the area as investments, which kept him in coin the rest of his life.

Apparently, Bill Antrim was ready to leave Wichita as well despite members of his family relocating there. Some accounts claim that Bill's brother James (who went on to become a well-respected citizen and popular law officer there) accompanied Bill and Catherine to Wichita in 1870. His parents and a sister arrived as the McCartys left.

CHAPTER THREE

CATCHING THE "FEVER"

"He was no more of a problem than any other boy growing up in a mining camp."

—MARY PATIENCE RICHARDS, HENRY'S
SCHOOLTEACHER

TO DENVER!

AND HOW DID THEY GET TO DENVER? THEY COULD HAVE TAKEN the train. The Kansas Pacific Railroad opened in 1870, running from Kansas City to Denver. However, having to pack for two growing boys, including their household goods and Catherine's washtubs (if she took them), more than likely filled a prairie schooner covered wagon. They would drive more than 520 miles west over ruts created by previous migrants.

Assuming they traveled by wagon, they would have traveled the Cherokee Route, which came out of Arkansas and across Kansas, following mainly the Santa Fe Trail to Bent's Fort near present-day La Junta, Colorado.

Bent's Fort

Established in 1838 by the Bent brothers, Charles (who served as New Mexico's territorial governor from 1846 to 1847) and William, plus Ceran St. Vrain, Bent's Fort was no fort in the military sense. Created more as a security and trading post than as a place for soldiers, the fort quickly grew into a resting place as well for fur trappers, merchants from the United States and Mexico, and Southern Cheyenne and Arapaho Plains Indians.

Set almost in the middle of the 900-mile Santa Fe Trail, travelers could buy ammunition and a wide variety of supplies (e.g., coffee, salt, and dried pork) and find other migrants who could share news. Socializing was almost as important as supplies. It was the only settlement on the Santa Fe Trail not under the jurisdiction and control of the Native Americans or Mexicans. Seeing the fort looming in the distance must have brought many easy breaths to the travelers.

Unfortunately, in 1849, a cholera epidemic hit the Indian population. Bent and his associates abandoned the fort, moving it north to Fort St. Vrain on the South Platte River. In 1853, Bent returned and built a stone fort on a bluff above Big Timbers and called it Bent's New Fort, conducting business until 1860.

Bent's "Old" Fort of today was built in 1976 during Colorado's centennial and is an exact replica based on archaeological evidence, paintings, sketches, and diaries. Located fifteen miles east of La Junta, Colorado, the fort is open to the public for a small fee.

That Cherokee Route, the one the McCarty/Antrim clan followed, was first used in 1849 and followed the Arkansas River to Pueblo, Colorado. It then struck due north on the route known as the Old Trapper's Trail. By modern highways, the route is U.S. 50 West from Wichita to Pueblo, then I-25 north to Denver. "This would be the most logical route because it was definitely the most used."[1]

Travel in the west in the 1870s was rough: no rest areas with toilets, running water, and vending machines; no fast-food joints to fill a hungry belly; and no overhead lights at night under which to sleep. Instead of averaging sixty miles *per hour* like today's vehicles, immigrants could hope for at most twenty miles *per day*. And travelers had to rely on their own experiences and those of others when setting out like the McCartys and Antrim did. Although limited, Indian attacks were still a concern as the Cheyenne, Sioux, Kiowa, Comanche, and Kaw roamed the Great Plains. They were not welcoming to migrants, a fact that kept settlers uneasy. However, after the army's winter campaign of 1868–1869, the worst of the Kansas Plains Indian warfare was over. Scattered incidents continued, but things were relatively calm on the Kansas frontier at that time. There was safety in numbers. Billy, known now as Henry, and his family did not travel alone.

What's in a Name?

It has been argued how Billy came to be known as Henry McCarty, but logically, it's simple. When Catherine teamed up with William Antrim, there were now two "Bills" in the household. One Billy and one Bill was one too many. More than likely, around this time, Catherine started calling her son by his middle name, Henry. Childhood friends in Silver City confirmed the Kid's real name was William. Those friends also added that the Kid never liked being referred to by his middle name but would answer to both Billy and Henry.

Despite what today we would call "hardships," to a growing boy, traveling across the plains must have been an adventure like no other. He and Josie walked, as most people did, while Antrim would have driven the oxen. Catherine would have walked when strong enough. The brothers would have been responsible for gathering buffalo chips and anything else to burn. They also would have had the chance to explore within sight of the wagons, chase prairie chickens, and enjoy the day. In the evenings, they would help Antrim water the horses and oxen, grease wagon wheels, haul water, and clean dishes.

Certainly, Antrim's previous experience as a teamster in Indianapolis would allow him to skillfully navigate across the shortgrass Great Plains.

Ah, the plains. One Santa Fe Trail traveler spoke of the "purity of the plains" and how it seemed to cure sickness. Surely, Catherine wanted that too.[2] Because there are few natural barriers, wind is normal for the North American prairie. Wind, along with grass, personified the Great Plains. Either by wagon or by train, Henry surely encountered bison along the way, even though their herd numbers were declining by then. He spotted grouse and certainly hundreds of prairie dogs. Add to that scorpions, snakes, a wide variety of birds, grasshoppers, pronghorn deer, and foxes.

Across the plains they went, arriving in Denver before the first true cold set in and the snow began. However, the four stayed only briefly.

Wells Fargo, founded in 1852 in New York City, offered plenty of employment opportunities in the West and could have been Antrim's incentive for relocating to Denver. The company's two-story Denver headquarters saw Concord coaches, overland stages, and horse-drawn wagons coming and going, hauling anything and everything, including eggs, oysters, and mining equipment.

In 1870, the Mile High City was a hustling, bustling town. After gold was discovered in 1858 at the confluence of Cherry Creek and the South Platte River, the encampment turned into a place of mass migration almost overnight. While mining was certainly a draw, people afflicted with tuberculosis and other

Denver in the 1870s. Named after Kansas Territorial Governor James W. Denver, the town sprung up after gold was found in 1858. Shortly after, it became the supply hub for new mines in the area.
AUTHOR'S COLLECTION

maladies arrived from all over for the clear, dry air of Colorado. Expensive resorts for consumptives sprung up throughout the area, offering hot baths and restorative treatment. Catherine, who most likely could not afford the exorbitantly priced resorts, could definitely partake of the dry, sunny climate and fresh, invigorating mountain air.[3]

HEADING SOUTH
The family didn't stay in Denver long. Instead, they chose to take the Santa Fe Trail south into Santa Fe. A train line ran south from Denver to Pueblo, but from there, the only route to Santa Fe was by the trail. A horse, a mule, an ox, or even a burro-drawn wagon or stage was their limited choice of transportation. From

Pueblo, the route first ran another eighty-five miles south through treeless prairies to the trading center of Trinidad, Colorado. Here, they joined the Mountain Branch of the Santa Fe Trail. Near the center of town, a grove of cottonwoods ran along the Purgatoire River, providing a shaded resting spot for travelers.

Eighteen miles south of Trinidad, they stopped at "Uncle" Dick Wootton's hotel and stagecoach stop at the base of the dreaded 7,834-foot Raton Pass. Often, Barlow and Sanderson's Southern Overland Mail and Express stagecoach passengers took the opportunity to freshen up at the hotel, enjoy a good meal, maybe have a drink, and sleep in a bed. Wootton owned the toll road over which everyone going north or south traversed. Cost for the stage passage would have been $1.50 ($32.57 today) per person.

Knowing they had to navigate over Raton Pass, which was close to impassable in winter, the foursome would have left Denver by the end of October 1872.

EPIZOOTIC CALAMITY

But weather wasn't the only problem faced when leaving Wichita. The summer of 1872 saw the worst epidemic of equine influenza in the nation's history. Originating in Ontario, Canada, it swept east to west during the winter of 1872–1873, and by the end of December, the Great Epizootic of 1872 had arrived in Colorado and New Mexico. This highly contagious disease was not usually fatal in otherwise healthy horses and mules (only about 1 percent died), but the malady debilitated them for weeks, causing extreme weakness, coughing, and general discomfort. Across the nation, transportation came to a standstill, demonstrating the reliance on horsepower.

It temporarily suspended transportation, trade, and commerce, ultimately causing a depression. Fire equipment stood unused without horsepower, which was partially responsible for the infamous fire that consumed Boston in November 1872. Firefighters were powerless to get their equipment on-site. Even voters were slowed on the eve of the reelection of President Ulysses S. Grant. Since the railroad had not made its way into southern Colorado and New Mexico, at this time, travel was highly restricted. Understandably, prices for stage and wagon travel skyrocketed. But somehow, the McCarty/Antrim party continued on.

TO SANTA FE!

Why choose Santa Fe, the end of the trail? Perhaps Antrim had heard about a lucrative mining opportunity there. We'll never know for sure. The four followed the busy commerce trail, successfully navigating the treacherous Raton Pass. On the trail, a wagon train could cover about fifteen to twenty miles per day. From Denver, the trip would have taken at least two weeks before arriving in the high-desert town.

Here, piñon and juniper–dotted hills gave way to the evergreen and aspen–laden Sangre de Cristo Mountains, which closed off Santa Fe to the north. Cornfields skirted the west, south, and east beyond the last dwellings. Prairie surrounded the west. No doubt, Henry looked forward to exploring the area.

Originally named La Villa Real de la Santa Fe de San Francisco de Asis by Spanish conquistadores, its name meant "The Royal City of the Holy Faith of Saint Francis of Assisi." The mouthful was reduced to "Santa Fe."

Coming into town, Henry and his family spotted rows of squat, brown buildings clumped along the relatively flat, treeless floodplain of the Santa Fe River. The capital city resembled "a dilapidated brick kiln or prairie-dog town."[4]

Whatever the McCarty clan thought of Santa Fe, records indicate no one named McCarty or Antrim stayed at the Exchange Hotel (where La Fonda now stands). The Exchange was the only hotel in town and was perched literally at the end of the trail. More than likely, Bill Antrim's sister, Mary Antrim Hollinger, let them stay at her house.

Once the horse equine flu subsided, commerce as well as entertainment picked up in lively Santa Fe. Numerous saloons, dance halls, and brothels held great appeal for locals and visitors alike. Travelers who had survived the deserts, the prairies, navigating Raton Pass, and the marauding Indians certainly enjoyed the gambling halls, where the game of keno went on day and night. Horse racing was big business, and Santa Fe provided. Heavy action took place along the Arroyo Mascaras just north of town with the sporting folk laying out a racecourse along the road to the mining district of Cerillos. This area was about three miles southwest of the plaza, and more important, it was flat.

Footraces in town drew crowds as well. Purses of $100 or more were won in these well-attended races along Lincoln Avenue. Some citizens objected to the races being run on Sundays, although they didn't mind if it was a race of the four-footed kind.

Santa Fe in 1873 was populated with a rich combination of Hispanic (many descendants of Spain's conquistadores), Mexican, Native American, and Anglo cultures. And within the Anglo culture, one would find people from all over the globe—immigrants from Ireland, England, Germany, Italy, Prussia, and so on who brought their customs and languages to the far reaches of the United States.

The New Mexico Territory was made up mostly of Hispanic and Mexican people who spoke mainly Spanish. Even today, there are communities in New Mexico where only Spanish is spoken. Within a matter of weeks of being fully immersed in the Spanish language and Hispanic/Mexican culture, Henry spoke Spanish like a native. He also learned about their relaxed lifestyle and customs. Men embraced each other, graciously welcomed guests into their homes where they lavished them with drinks and food, and showed high respect for older and younger people. And if that wasn't enough, women were allowed many more freedoms than "back in the States." Women drank, smoked, gambled, and owned their own businesses. Undoubtedly, Catherine found kindred spirits in this vast outpost called New Mexico.

Hispanic *fandangos* and *bailes* took place almost every night. More Americans coming into town brought more American dances, including masked balls and a social "hop" at Fort Marcy. Immediately, Henry fell in love with the *bailes*. As an adult, he often traveled miles to attend one where Mexican musicians played their violins, *guitarróns*, *vihuelas*, and sometimes harps and coronets. Surely, Henry and his mother attended these dances.

One custom during the dance was that señoritas could seek the favor of a young man by smashing *cascarones* (eggshells filled with perfumed confetti) over their heads. It was all fun.

Indeed, Santa Fe was a lively town.

Catherine's health must have improved in the high, thin air, leaving her well enough to marry Antrim. According to Santa Fe law, a couple had to show proof of at least three weeks' residency prior to getting married. For a few months before the wedding, the McCartys and Antrim probably lived in town with Antrim's sister. One must wonder why she was not signed as a witness to the marriage. Surely, she was in attendance. Possibly, she did not actually reside in town (records are sketchy) and the four, instead, lived at the Exchange Hotel under an alias, as cohabitating without marriage was against the law.

We know for sure Henry McCarty was in Santa Fe, New Mexico Territory, on March 1, 1873, when, at the tender age of twelve, he stood with his brother Josie (maybe nine) as witness to his mother's marriage. Under azure skies, the simple ceremony at the First Presbyterian Church on the corner of Grant and Griffin streets was led by the Reverend D. F. McFarland, uniting the widow Catherine (née Devine) McCarty, age forty-three, to William Henry Harrison Antrim, age thirty. Embellished by piñon and juniper aromas from fires in nearby homes, southwestern smells carried by early spring breezes wafted across the land.

Reverend McFarland (who retired due to ill health at the end of the year)
administered the vows at the First Presbyterian Church on the corner of
Grant and Griffin streets. Originally a Baptist mission and the first Protestant church in the territory, it was abandoned at some point. In 1867, the
Presbyterians bought the property and added a square tower and gothic
windows.

According to both church and Santa Fe County records, five people witnessed the union: Amanda McFarland, the minister's wife; Katie McFarland, the minister's daughter; Harvey Edmonds, a local citizen who often acted as witness to marriages; and, scrawled in the ledger in the minister's own hand, William H. McCarty and Joseph McCarty.

It's hardly speculation to assume that young Henry's emotions must have run the gamut from hating Antrim for breaking up the McCarty threesome to being overjoyed at completing the family. This was likely the first time Henry had a real "father." Antrim was a grown man, someone he could look up to, to emulate. He must have looked forward to many years of having a dad—fishing, hunting, and driving wagons together—everything a boy could want in a father.

After the wedding, the new family may have rented a house or perhaps one or two rooms at a boardinghouse or stayed with Antrim's sister. Some historians believe the new family moved into the Exchange Hotel across the street from the town's plaza, but again, records say otherwise.

What did they do to make a living? Records are sketchy, but with Antrim's teamster experience and Catherine's laundry business and selling baked goods, they may have done enough to stay afloat. Henry supposedly washed dishes at the Exchange Hotel, which everyone called "La Fonda," meaning "The Inn." In his free time, Henry played the piano in the lobby.[5] Having a beautiful tenor voice even as a youngster, he sang on the street and made extra money.

The Exchange Hotel

The Exchange Hotel was literally at the end of the Santa Fe Trail. In 1922, after tearing down the Exchange, a third hotel was built on that site. City records indicate that today's

La Fonda sits on the site of the town's first inn, established when the city was founded by Spaniards in 1607, making this property the oldest hotel corner in America. Several U.S. presidents have stayed there, including Ulysses S. Grant and John F. Kennedy. In 1925, Fred Harvey made it into the Harvey House. La Fonda today features a unique blend of southwestern and art deco styles. La Fonda is open for business today.

Henry would have enjoyed today's La Fonda Hotel with the bands that come in to play. Some of the top names in the country have performed there, including actor Wes Studi and his band.

Records do not mention Henry ever learning to play piano well, but his love of music was evident from an early age. Documented by his friends and newspaper articles, his forays into song, dance, harmonica playing, and acting defined this youngster. His mother, who loved to sing and dance, had influenced her son by giving him the gift of music.

CHAPTER FOUR

HALCYON DAYS IN SILVER CITY

*"Billy was a graceful and beautiful dancer, and when in the
company of a woman, he was at all times extremely polite and
respectful."*

—NEW MEXICO TERRITORY
GOVERNOR MIGUEL A. OTERO

ON THE MOVE AGAIN

By FEBRUARY 1873, THE GREAT EPIZOOTIC, WHICH HAD CAUSED
upheaval for the transportation business, had run its course.
Recovered, horses and mules pulled wagons once again, and stages
began arriving in Santa Fe from over Raton Pass and up from
Albuquerque. On the human end, another type of malady, "dia-
mond fever" (a catchall phrase for gold craziness), was taking the
country by storm. The lure of gold, copper, and silver was a siren
song for migrants in the United States as well as for immigrants
from the rest of the world.

Across the nation, gold fever was at a pitch, and Bill Antrim
had it bad—if not worse than many others. The hills and mountains in southwestern New Mexico and eastern Arizona touted
silver and gold deposits, wide veins of those precious metals ripe

for the picking. Eastern newspapers claimed nuggets lay right on the ground; mining was that easy. Men and women from around the world rushed to the territory.

The newly minted Antrim family, both boys taking Antrim as a last name, left Santa Fe. Where could they go that had clear, clean air for Catherine's lungs and enough mountains to satisfy Antrim's mining obsession? The Black Range of New Mexico seemed to fit the bill.

Soon after the wedding, the Antrims loaded into a wagon or stagecoach and moved 150 miles south and a bit west of Santa Fe to the mining camp of Georgetown, New Mexico Territory, located between Piños Altos and Silver City. Georgetown, founded in 1872, mined mainly silver and flourished from 1876 to 1886. When the Antrims moved in, the town was nothing but a rough-and-tumble camp.

While Antrim was delighted to be in Georgetown, Catherine was not. She sought a decent place in which to raise her sons, somewhere with a school and stores, an established town with a sense of community. Many signs pointed to southwestern New Mexico Territory, where good employment prospects awaited along with a chance for Antrim to strike it rich. He begrudgingly agreed to move the family eighteen miles south to Silver City.

Nestled in the Black Range foothills, Silver City, known as La Ciénaga de San Vicente, was home to generations of Mexican miners and settlers. Before them, Chiricahua Apache had been living in the area since the 1400s and had declared war on anyone encroaching on their hunting territory. Spain owned the area until 1821, after which Mexico took control until 1846. Around 1800, an Apache showed a Spanish officer where his tribe had been mining pure veins of native copper. The Spaniards got the "fever," extracting many thousands of tons of pure copper. The ore was then transported by mule train to Chihuahua, where it was stamped into coinage. During the 1820s and 1830s, Apache raided the area so frequently, attempting to regain their hunting

today's

grounds, that the owner of the major mine had to build a fort to protect his men.

In 1846, when U.S. General Stephen Watts Kearny and his Army of the West rode into Santa Fe and declared this part of the Southwest now to be under U.S. rule, the floodgates were opened for miners believing in Manifest Destiny. In 1870, a large deposit of silver was discovered about ten miles from Silver City, leading to the city's founding. The first Anglo settler arrived in 1871, and by year's end, the village had blossomed into eighty buildings. Over a short period of time, Silver City became the commercial hub for all mining activity throughout the area.

By 1873, when the Antrims moved in, the community prided itself on "eastern" lodgings and had a mainly Anglo feel. Unlike any other territory town crowded with thick adobe buildings, this was a well-structured and surprisingly progressive community. Silver City spread across a broad valley on the downslope between two hillsides. Two-story buildings made of red brick stood next

Silver City, ca. 1872. Silver City, a town built to last, is the oldest unincorporated town in New Mexico and the only one still operating under a territorial charter. It boasts the oldest public school system in the state. Its historic neighborhoods tell the stories of its visionary founders.

PHOTO COURTESY OF THE SILVER CITY MUSEUM

35

to sunbaked adobes and log cabins. Mercantiles, livery stables, saloons, restaurants, a bowling alley, dance halls, butcher shops, an apothecary, a post office, a furniture store, and various other commercial stores marched up and down the center of town. The hustle and bustle of stagecoaches, freight wagons, prairie schooners, wagons, and buggies filled the valley. South of town, stamp mills pulverized ore hauled in from as far away as Arizona and Mexico, adding to the commotion.

Silver City boomed, growing day by day. The Antrims were part of the surge in population that grew Silver City from 900 to almost 2,000 residents in three years. "The booming migration created a shortage of drinking water and housing so severe that the local barber, P. Wagner, had to stop selling baths and turn his fenced yard into a campground for newcomers living in their tents."[1] In 1873, most new families were living in tents. Antrim had been lucky to buy a tiny cabin, thought to be one of the original structures, on Main Street and Broadway. It stood next to what they called the "Big Ditch," a streambed beside the main thoroughfare that carried runoff from mountain storms. (A series of floods in 1895 scooped out Main Street, sweeping away all the buildings, including Antrim's cabin.) Glad to have a sturdy roof over their heads and log walls to keep out the weather, Catherine knew the small log cabin would have to do until they could buy a town plot and, it was hoped, build a larger house. Being a loving wife and mother, conscientious Catherine was able to make a decent home out of the crowded cabin.

Seeking opportunity for building a larger house, Antrim filed on lots 4 and 6, block 16, of the R. M. Kidder plat on June 10, 1874, a year after moving to town. Unfortunately, the house would never be built.

As she had in Wichita, Catherine wasted no time settling down and getting to work. She once again offered her laundry-cleaning service; baked and sold cakes, pies, and bread; and took in boarders. Yes, even in her tiny cabin. One of those who boarded at the Antrim cabin was Ash Upson (cowriter of Pat Garrett's *The Authentic Life of Billy the Kid*), who would provide one of the more vivid descriptions of Catherine Antrim:

> *To those who knew Billy the Kid's mother, her courteous, kindly, and benevolent spirit was no mystery. She was evidently of Irish descent. Her husband called her Kathleen. She was about medium height, straight and graceful in form, with regular features, light blue eyes, and luxuriant golden hair. She was not a beauty, but what the world calls a fine-looking woman. She kept boarders in Silver City, and her charity and goodness of heart was proverbial. Many a hungry tenderfoot has had cause to bless the fortune which led him to her door. In all her deportment she exhibited the unmistakable characteristics of a lady—a lady by instinct and education.*[2]

Neighbors remembered Catherine with fondness and recalled her vivacious and outgoing personality along with her love of dancing, which she passed on to her elder son. She often took Henry with her to dance halls, and folks remembered her as one of the best dancers in town.

Catherine's health seemed to be improving. She and Henry enthusiastically joined in the *bailes*, held on Monday, Wednesday, Saturday, and Sunday nights in the dance halls, which usually were part of a saloon. One such place, McGary's Hall on North Main, doubled as the first church and first courthouse. In Ward's Hall, only men entered from the front; women and children went in through the back. Dances cost fifty cents each. Twenty-five cents went to the house and the rest to the musicians who would play tunes such as "The American Traveler," "Fisher's Hornpipe," and "The Irish Washerwoman." Henry loved "Turkey in the Straw" and frequently requested the *gallina* (chicken) song, as he called it.

In the Hispanic section of town, public *bailes* were held in large *salas* or reception rooms, where dancers changed partners often. Popular dances included waltz, schottische, polka, and an assortment of regional dances.[3] Musicians with violins, harps, guitars, horns, and sometimes an Indian *tombe*, or drums, played from a raised platform where spectators took seats on both sides of the *sala*.

No matter where Catherine and Henry danced, they enjoyed themselves. One observer said, "Mrs. Antrim could dance the Highland Fling as well as the best of the dancers."[4]

Neighbors remember Catherine as a jolly Irish lady, full of life and mischief. Despite her illness, she showed fortitude and good cheer, traits evident also in Henry.

THE MUSIC MAN

Much to Catherine's pleasure, she was able to send her boys to school in Silver City. March 28, 1874, marked the end of the first semester of public school for Henry and Josie. Concerned about keeping the youngsters busy and out of trouble, the editor of the local newspaper recommended the children form a theatrical troupe. Proceeds from the shows would help raise money for a real schoolhouse for the thirty students who attended the first session. In preparation for the summer school session, a run-down adobe house was cleaned and repaired to be used as a makeshift school. It served well until the roof collapsed, sending mud and debris onto students' heads during a heavy August rainstorm. The teacher, Mrs. Pratt, immediately quit and left the area.

Henry loved the idea of performing. He got busy putting together actors and props, doing a bit of directing. The youngsters' morality plays, such as Harriet Beecher Stowe's *Uncle Tom's Cabin* and T. S. Arthur's *Ten Nights in a Barroom*, were held in meeting and dance halls. Beginning as ragtag creations, the troupe eventually smoothed into creating full-scale theatrical productions. "Billy was Head Man in the show," commented a fellow thespian.[5]

Since one of the purposes of this endeavor was to raise money for public school, we can add to his list of achievements that *Billy the Kid helped raise money for the first organized public school system in New Mexico.*

Not only did Henry perform in school plays, he also sang in Spanish and danced to Spanish folk songs. Henry was captivated by music, and he played the harmonica. The first time he heard "Silver Threads among the Gold," a newly written ode to a sweetheart, Henry was taken with the heartfelt lyrics and sentimental music. He declared the piece his favorite, supplanting the old fiddle tune "Turkey in the Straw," derived from an Irish ballad. He often whistled "Silver Threads" as he rode across Lincoln County and the Texas panhandle rustling cattle.

Henry was known for dressing well. Everyone commented on his neat appearance and clean habits. Courteous almost to a fault, especially to the ladies and older people, he had an alert mind, read and wrote better than many adults, and had a rambunctious sense of humor, often making jokes at his own expense. Although small in stature, for which he took a lot of ribbing, Henry had tremendous energy and quick reflexes. "Anxious to please, eager to impress, willing to take extraordinary risks, [Henry] would dare anything to prove his worth. The other schoolkids soon realized that he had genuine courage."[6]

In addition to singing and dancing, Henry was an avid reader. The moment chores were done, he'd sprawl out somewhere with a book. Eventually, adventure books and dime novels gave way to the *Police Gazette*, which may have inspired his future forays into lawlessness.

"He was quiet, I remember," related Chauncey Truesdell, Henry's friend, "and never swore or tried to act bad like the other kids."[7]

A year passed, and living in Silver City was going well for the family. They had a house to call home while many families were still living in tents or camps outside of town. Henry and his brother attended school and had other children to play with. After school, the Antrim boys and their gaggle of friends headed straight for the tiny cabin, where they played games of foot racing and pirates until suppertime. Catherine always had a full cookie jar waiting for the boys when they came home.

A NEW DAY

On September 14, 1874, thirteen-year-old Henry and eleven-year-old Josie started the fall school semester under the instruction of a new teacher. Mary Patience Richards was twenty-five years old, elegant, and educated in England. Her accent may have reminded Henry of his ma. Richards recalled Henry as "a scrawny little fellow with delicate hands and an artistic nature. [He was] always willing to help with the chores around the schoolhouse. Henry was no more of a problem in school than any other boy growing up in a mining camp."[8]

Ms. Richards and Henry shared an unusual talent: both were ambidextrous. Henry could write just as well with his left hand as he did with his right. He confided to friends that because of that, he and Ms. Richards had to be related.

Young Henry McCarty adapted quite well to his new home and excelled in school. He is known to have been an excellent student at the top of his class.

"[Henry] was one of the best boys in town," recalled Tony Conner, one of Henry's close friends. "He was very slender. He was undersized and was really girlish looking. I never remember [him] doing anything out of the way any more than the rest of us." He added, "We had our chores to do, like washing dishes and other duties around the house."[9]

Remembrances of Henry in Silver City depict him not as an unusual youth but as a lively teenager who attended school, loved and respected his mother, and got along with his stepfather. Some recalled his mischievous ways, his smiling face, and his prominent two front teeth.

But it wasn't Henry's oversized teeth that set him apart from other boys; it was his eyes. They were constantly on the move, always looking, taking in the scenery, wiggling. Silver City Sheriff Harvey H. Whitehill, the first lawman to arrest him, noted, "There was one peculiar facial characteristic that to an experienced manhunter, would have marked him as a bad man. . . . And that was his dancing eyes. They were never at rest, but continually shifted and roved, much like his own rebellious nature."[10]

With a small but steady income from Catherine's and Antrim's labors, the family was getting by financially. Antrim received an income from properties rented in Wichita, and he worked as a carpenter and a butcher in Richard Knight's meat market. But records show he did little to support his family. Some neighbors remembered Bill Antrim as a hardworking man but notoriously stingy with his money. Mining was not a profitable venture for inexperienced prospectors. Despite his penchant for being "frugal," he would spend hours in saloons gambling what little money he did have. Like other men in Silver City, he bet heavily on card games and faro while setting out to learn the rudiments of mining. He did, however, find time to travel to the mines at Chloride Flat, Georgetown, and Piños Altos and the Carlisle mines near the Arizona border. He was often absent for long periods of time mining.

Catherine continued to make ends meet by taking in laundry, baking, feeding, and taking care of boarders in the already crowded cabin.

The stress of physical labor and emotional strain caused Catherine's health to worsen. Those suffering from tuberculosis are plagued not only with hacking coughs and chest pains but also with severe fatigue, making rest and a stress-free lifestyle essential. But Catherine was not getting that. She had two boys to support.

A friend suggested to Catherine that she should go to Hudson Hot Springs, a lush high-desert oasis twenty-six miles southeast of Silver City near Ojo Caliente. The warm, bubbling sulfur baths were thought to cure patients of all kinds of illnesses. People flocked there, enjoying days lounging in the warm water.

Unfortunately, the hot-water baths did not improve Catherine's health, and she was soon bedridden. A neighbor, Clara Truesdell, a graduate of nursing school and mother of Chauncey (one of Henry's friends), tended to Catherine and also took care of Henry and Josie. Chauncey recounted how Billy would always sit at his mother's side, hold her hand, and try to comfort her during her painful coughing attacks.

Chimney smelter furnaces south of town belched acrid smoke continually, covering the lower half of town, blocking the clean air Catherine McCarty Antrim so desperately needed. Her health was failing, and it seemed the sicker she got, the longer Antrim was absent. Catherine's health deteriorated rapidly. She was bedridden for almost four months until her death. The fact that Antrim was not there for his dying wife and to support his young stepsons, emotionally and financially, does not speak well for him.

In fact, a few months before her death, Antrim sold both lots on which he had planned to build a house to Joseph Buhlman, who wanted to open a shoe store.[11]

Catherine understandably felt abandoned and correctly prophesied her sons would be neglected after she was gone. One day, Catherine told her friend Clara how concerned she was about what would happen to her sons. Grieving for Catherine, Clara promised that she would look after the precious boys.

CHAPTER FIVE

THE DAY THE MUSIC DIED

"He had a mind whose ingenuity we knew not of at that time.
He was only a boy, you must remember, scarcely over 15 years
of age."

—SILVER CITY SHERIFF HARVEY WHITEHILL

CATHERINE'S LEGACY

ON SEPTEMBER 16, 1874, AFTER ALMOST FOUR MONTHS IN BED
and nineteen months of marriage to Bill Antrim, forty-five-year-
old Catherine Antrim took her last ragged breath. Her husband
had again disappeared into the hills for prospecting and could not
be found. Nor was he there for his wife's funeral or to give comfort
to his grieving stepsons.

Henry was thirteen.

The day after Catherine's death, Clara Truesdell prepared the
body for burial as family friend David Abraham made the coffin
and his son dug the grave. The service itself was held at the Antrim cabin, and many of the neighbors attended. As there was no
hearse in town, David Abraham transported her body in his own
surrey several blocks to the cemetery. Walking alone down the dirt
road, Henry and Josie followed behind the surrey. Catherine was
laid to rest, and a simple wooden cross marked her grave.

Her death proved catastrophic for Henry and Josie.

Henry's world had been pulled out from under him. Feeling all alone (and rightfully so), he struggled to find a thread of normalcy to hang on to. He and Josie returned to school, where Ms. Richards took Henry under her wing. It's not clear where the boys stayed in the weeks after their mother's death until Antrim's return, though it was probably with the Truesdells.

At long last, Bill Antrim found his way home. Perhaps he was the one who made the wooden cross for Catherine's grave. The marker lasted several years until either torn down or swept away in a torrential rainstorm.

Then Antrim sold the cabin and placed his stepsons with his former employer, butcher Richard Knight, and left Silver City for Arizona.

Antrim was not a mean man as some historians try to claim. He understood how to do a day's work, but he had no idea how to raise someone else's children, especially teenaged boys. He did not have a relationship with either of his step-sons. Nor was he inclined to spend his money supporting them. So he

Bill Antrim left both Henry and Josie to fend for themselves in Silver City after Catherine died. Photo is at the Confidence mine in Mogollon, New Mexico, 1890s.

AUTHOR'S COLLECTION

did what he thought was best. He found a place for them to stay and then walked away.

Near the end of 1874, Henry and Josie were separated. Knight sent Henry to live with the Truesdells. Surely, he clung to that family as a lifeline—people he knew and who had liked his ma. Henry thought of Clara as a second mother; she had been Catherine's best friend. Chauncey Truesdell was one of his best friends. The family had recently bought the Star Hotel on Hudson Street, renovated the business, and renamed it the Exchange Hotel (a quite popular name in the West).

It's not hard to imagine the thoughts and feelings Henry experienced. At the tender age of thirteen, right when he needed adult supervision and guidance most, he was on his own. Issues of abandonment by Antrim, loss of his mother and all the nurturing she'd given, and even not seeing his brother Josie every day surely spun this orphan into a tailspin. While he knew right from wrong, still he needed guidance but received none.

More and more often, he thought of ways to get money. After all, not only was he growing, but he enjoyed looking well dressed. He needed clothes. Henry plotted and planned after spotting costume jewelry on display in a storefront. The baubles were destined to be raffled off by a Mexican circus passing through town. Henry convinced his friend Charlie Stevens to go in with him, planning to grab the plunder, then hightail it to Mexico and sell it for a huge profit.

However, before the robbery, Charlie grew cold feet and told his father, who marched his son down to the owner's store to repeat what he'd been a part of. Immediately, Charlie's father and the store's owner gave Henry a stern talking to. Henry promised not to do it again and to earn money fair and square.

And he did that. Thirteen-year-old, smooth-cheeked, blue-eyed Henry worked in the Truesdell's Exchange Hotel, washing dishes and waiting tables at the restaurant to pay for his room and board. He was reported to be very friendly, and the manager boasted that Henry was the only kid who ever worked for him who didn't steal anything.

Henry's brother Josie was sent to live with Joe Dyer, a proprietor of the New Orleans Club. Josie, now around eleven years old, worked for his keep at the saloon, cleaning, serving liquor, and running errands. Unfortunately, growing up in such an environment without any parental supervision or guidance, Josie also gambled, drank, and was even spotted by a childhood friend smoking at a Chinese opium den. Within a couple of years, Josie was thoroughly submerged into this world.

Bill Antrim stayed in Arizona most of the time, mining for that elusive metal. However, he continued to come and go from Silver City without any regular contact with his stepsons. Apparently, he felt he had done all he could do and discharged his parental duties.

Although they were living in different homes, Henry and Josie saw each other around town and in school. When not in school or working, Henry spent more and more time learning the fine art of card playing, dealing monte and faro. A quick study, he soon became adept at the games.

BECOMING A "VILLAGE ARAB"

When not in school or church or at work, Henry and his friends did what teenagers do—anything except what they are supposed to. Owen L. Scott, the editor of *Mining Life*, a Silver City newspaper, kept a close watch on the town's children. Fed up with their shenanigans, the editor dubbed the kids the "Village Arabs," a term used back East for vagabond children or homeless orphans, and took delight in reporting their every misstep. After school, the "Arabs" would set up a racecourse near the newspaper's office and race their "horses." One of the teens would be the horse, and the children would bet on the various racers. Henry, being small, raced alongside the others. The antics were loud and boisterous up and down Market Street.

When a large Mexican circus came to town, the Arabs followed the parade of entertainers as they entered downtown. The older teens even performed daring tricks of their own, much to the delight of younger Arabs.

AND SO, TROUBLE BEGINS

Henry experienced a sliver of family stability living with the Truesdells, but this was short lived. During the summer of 1875, the Truesdells began experiencing domestic issues. Henry was in the way and needed to leave; what was left of his tenuous world was pulled out from under him. Henry was sent to live with Mrs. Sarah Brown in her boardinghouse. Although no longer living with them, he remained close friends with Chauncey and Clara Truesdell.

Without his stepfather or any kind of adult guidance, Henry was forced to fend for himself and began to get into trouble.

"He was a good kid," declared friend Louis Abraham, "but he got in [with] the wrong company."[1]

To make money, Henry worked at Richard Knight's butcher shop and with Knight's competitor, City Meat Market. His job consisted of killing the steers, gutting, and skinning the carcasses, then chopping them into salable meat.

For additional income, Henry took up gambling. Men in that day bet on almost anything, ranging from cockfights to the weather. Therefore, residents accepted Henry's gambling as a legitimate way to make money. He was a quick study, having learned from Bill Antrim before he left town, and soon he became one of the best cardsharps around. Henry's small size, soft voice, and youthful looks lulled many of the gamblers into thinking they could beat him handily. Many card players walked away with empty pockets. Henry had learned well.

But gambling didn't pay the bills or put enough coin in his pocket. Despite his promise to stay out of trouble and not steal, Henry found the vow impossible to uphold. At such a young age, he turned to larceny. His first offense was the theft of several pounds of butter from a rancher who lived near Silver City.

Henry resold the butter to one of the local merchants. The butter's owner came to town and reported the theft. Henry's guilt was easily established, but after a stern talking to by newly appointed Silver City sheriff Harvey H. Whitehill, a large man with a booming voice and kindly disposition, Henry promised never to steal again. He was released.

Silver City Sheriff Harvey Whitehill was the first lawman to arrest Billy.
AUTHOR'S COLLECTION

This theft demonstrated how desperate Henry was to make money. Completely alone, except for his younger brother, whom he rarely saw now and who certainly gave him no advice, Henry clawed and scratched his way through the next few months. Friends observed how poverty had pulled him into larceny. "He was a little mischievous at times," admitted his friend Louis Abraham. "More than the rest of us with a little more nerve."[2]

And Henry had a lot of nerve. Once when his employer, City Meat Market owner Charles Bottom, took sick, Henry talked him into letting him ride his "fine racing mare" through hazardous Indian country to retrieve medicinal cherry bark, thought to be a cure for high fever and chills. Henry saddled up and made the twenty-eight-mile round-trip in a day, returning with the bark and demonstrating that nerve—and compassion.

"SOMBRERO JACK DONE THE STEALING WHILST HENRY DONE THE HIDING"[3]

In desperate need of money for food and clothing, Henry took up with fellow boarder George Schaefer, locally known as "Sombrero

Jack" because he wore a broad-brimmed Mexican hat. George was older and bigger than Henry but someone Henry admired. According to the sheriff's son, who was a good friend of Henry, "Every Saturday night, George would get drunk. But he thought a lot of [Henry] and [Henry] used to follow him around. This fellow George liked to steal; he had a mania to steal and was always stealing."[4]

On September 4, 1875, a year after Catherine McCarty Antrim's death, drunken George broke into Charlie Sun's Chinese laundry, making off with an armload of clean clothes, two revolvers, and a large bundle of blankets belonging to townsfolk valued from $150 to $200 ($3,722 to $4,963). Hiding the stolen goods in Georgetown at the shutdown stamp pit at Crawford's Mill, Sombrero Jack realized he would need to move the items to a safer place. He knew Henry was poor and needed better clothes. So, in exchange for some clothes and a share of the profit, he suggested Henry hide the loot in his room until he could sell the goods.

Sounded like a good deal to Henry. Breaking his promise to the sheriff to be law abiding, he hid the clothes in a trunk in his room.

Unfortunately, on September 23, Mrs. Brown was cleaning Henry's room and discovered the stolen clothes. She ran to Sheriff Whitehill, reporting Henry had stolen property and was even wearing some of the garments. The sheriff tracked down Henry, giving Sombrero Jack time to skip town and disappear into Mexico.

Henry told his story at a hearing before the justice of the peace. The justice and the sheriff believed Henry was simply Sombrero Jack's fall guy.

Sheriff Whitehill sympathized with Henry, knowing his own sons were just as bad if not worse. "I did all I could for the orphaned boy," said Whitehill. "After all, he was somebody's son and a boy who didn't need to go wrong."[5] However, Whitehill decided to teach the youngster a lesson, perhaps hoping it would benefit his own children, too. Henry was charged with larceny, and he would remain in jail until his trial before the grand jury when the circuit court came to town the third week of November.

Mrs. Whitehill and the sheriff's visiting niece were outraged and appalled at the turn of events. The niece reported that her uncle told the family, "[Henry] was getting so wild after his mother's death, that [the sheriff] thought that by locking him up for the night it might get Henry to thinking and possibly do him some good."[6]

Mrs. Whitehill, who was very fond of Henry, insisted her husband bring him home for breakfast. Sheriff Whitehill had planned more than that. He figured that after giving Henry a few days behind bars to ponder his life, he'd turn him loose. He would even offer to let Henry stay at the Whitehill home, especially since the children were friends.

"[The crime] did not amount to anything," said Henry's close friend, Anthony Conner, "and Mr. Whitehill only wished to scare him."[7]

The sheriff's son agreed, "He didn't want to put him in a cell. He was just a boy who had stole some clothes. . . . He didn't want to be mean."[8]

Being jailed scared Henry all right. That much of his incarceration worked. However small the crime may have been, Henry took being locked up quite seriously. He figured he'd spend years behind bars simply for helping hide clothes. This was no way to live his life, he thought. However, he had no clue that Whitehill and the judge were trying to make a point and that they'd let him out of jail in a day or two. He'd stay locked up long enough to make an impact and keep him out of further trouble. However, with the combination of cunning and sincerity that marked his later escapades, after a day or two, he persuaded the sheriff to let him have the run of the corridor outside the cell, complaining the jailer was treating him roughly.

"And right there is where we fell down," conceded Whitehill. The sheriff left the boy unguarded for half an hour. "When we returned and unlocked the heavy oaken doors of the jail, the 'Kid' was nowhere to be seen."[9] Sheriff Whitehill searched everywhere and finally ran outside, where a man standing nearby reported that a kid had popped out of the chimney.

"The chimney hole did not appear as large as my arm," Whitehill said, "yet the lad squeezed his frail, slender body through it and gained his liberty."[10] In Sheriff Whitehill's opinion, it was then that William Henry McCarty Antrim began a career in lawlessness.

"He was not bad," Louis Abraham insisted. "He was just scared. If he had only waited until they let him out, he would have been alright, but he was scared and he ran away."[11]

ESCAPE TO NOWHERE

Many accounts speculate about Henry's flight from Silver City, ranging from that he was assisted by his stepfather to that he was hiding out at a sawmill. The most logical story is that after escaping up the chimney, Henry, who was soot covered, hightailed it to Mrs. Clara Truesdell, his surrogate mom. She cleaned him up, packed him a lunch, gave him as much money as she could, and flagged down a passing stagecoach headed for Globe, Arizona. He climbed on board hoping to find his stepfather somewhere in the next territory and waved adios to everything he knew.

Josie was probably sorry to hear of his brother's arrest but was cheering for him when he learned he had escaped. It would be almost two years before the brothers would see each other again for the last time.

Henry, now fleeing the authorities and completely on his own, had crossed that proverbial line, making life's profound decisions at an immature age. Without family, community, or a single person he knew and trusted, he was rushing headlong into a whole lot of unknown. Escaping was risky, but would it keep him out of jail? Now what? Where would he go? What would he do? He'd have to live by his wits and survival skills.

A risk taker to the point of foolhardiness and self-confident enough to believe things would work out, Henry was at least a pragmatist, trying on various jobs and lifestyles until one fit.

The William Henry McCarty Antrim of Silver City was morphing into the Kid.

Chapter Six

THE MAKING OF THE KID

"If Henry had had a mother to guide him, a father to teach him right from wrong and give him a profession, Henry would never have been Billy the Kid."

—MICHAEL WALLIS, AUTHOR OF
BILLY THE KID: THE ENDLESS RIDE

ESCAPE TO ARIZONA, 1875

HENRY HEADED FOR ARIZONA SEEKING OUT THE ONLY PERSON he thought would help: Bill Antrim. Would his stepfather take him in? Give him guidance and money? Keep him safe from the posse that was surely following?

What Henry didn't realize was that his crime and subsequent escape weren't especially noteworthy. Nobody from Silver City lit out after him. Nobody bothered to notify sheriffs in surrounding towns. It simply wasn't a big enough deal. Except to Henry.

After weeks of inquiries and drifting, he located Antrim 100 miles west of Silver City in Clifton, Arizona. Ironically, several Silver City residents, Sheriff Henry Whitehill, the Truesdells, and Richard Knight also owned or worked mines near Clifton, traveling there frequently.

Once he found Antrim, the reunion didn't go as hoped. After explaining the situation, Henry probably expected sympathy and help. Instead, Antrim's response was, "If that's the kind of boy you are, then get out."[1]

Left without any sort of kindness, Henry stole Antrim's six-shooter and some clothes. With the final proverbial safety net yanked out from under him, Henry left.

Without money, a job, or connections of any sort, Henry roamed Arizona's San Simon Valley and turned to what he knew best—gambling. He dealt cards in Safford and Pueblo Viejo as well as Camp Goodwin. When gambling didn't pay the bills, he became a saddle tramp, drifting from ranch to fort to camp in southern Arizona. He found temporary jobs on ranches along the Gila River doing seasonal work, such as gathering hay or herding cattle.

Along the way, he worked with tough ranch hands who easily tossed hay and performed other muscled jobs. He had trouble keeping up because of his size. He was a lightweight, one fore-man had said. Somewhere during this time, Henry was given the moniker "Kid." He worked for a while at the famous Henry H. Hooker ranch (Hooker was friends with Wyatt Earp), about six miles southwest of the post, but couldn't handle the physically demanding work.

Although not good at physical labor, Henry was smart and a quick learner of horsemanship and gunmanship, part of the western culture. Soon, horses and guns became an obsession with Henry.

Code of the West

The Code of the West dictated that a man did not have to back away from a fight. And he could pursue his adversary until the threat was over, even if it resulted in death. "Stand your ground" was a popular saying. The code set an ultrahigh value on courage (some called it bravado).

In this code, it was expected that every man had to ride well and shoot well.

Also in the code is to "ride for the brand," which not only implies loyalty to your outfit or employer but also assumes the cowboy/employee will go the extra mile to do the job. Whatever your boss says goes. You back his play even if you don't agree with it.

Although most of his life centered around gambling and carousing, Henry rarely drank or used tobacco despite the saloons offering plenty of opportunities. His nights at the saloon were spent enjoying time with his friends, singing, dancing, and gambling. Particularly expert at monte, he eventually achieved somewhat of a reputation as a monte dealer. Commercial whoring did not interest fifteen-year-old Henry. But what *did* interest him were the younger Hispanic señoritas. His good looks and charm worked wonders on many of them.

After being fired from his job as a ranch hand, Henry wandered toward the Camp Grant area in the Sulphur Springs Valley, where he dealt cards and gambled. He also worked at the Hotel de Luna inside the Camp Grant military reservation. Owned by Canadian Miles L. Wood, the four-room adobe hostelry provided a civilian respite with beds and meals.

Because of the nearby ranches and military taking all available help, hired hands were hard to come by. When Billy came looking for work, he was hired immediately—as cook and busboy. One can only imagine what he cooked since he had no prior experience, only his mother's culinary skills as a memory. It's questionable if she ever shared her recipes or if the young boy even paid attention when she tried to teach her son the ways around a kitchen.

Near the military camp's perimeter was Francis P. "Windy" Cahill's blacksmith shop. Cahill received his nickname "because he was always blowin' about one thing or another," reported Gus

At Camp Grant in Arizona, Billy worked as a cook and dish "swabber" at the Hotel de Luna around 1875.

Gildea, a cowboy who had ridden in with one of John Chisum's herd.[2] Henry would pass by Windy's shop almost daily, and certainly Windy ate some of Henry's cooking. Windy would feature prominently in Henry's future.

When not cooking, Billy honed his card skills and built a reputation as a cardsharp. He also realized that with his small size, the only equalizer in gambling disagreements was a Colt handgun. Colt's motto: "God created men equal. Colonel Colt *made* them equal." He practiced shooting daily.

At some point, Henry decided neither "Kid," "Billy," nor "Henry" were appropriate monikers for such a man as he. Touting himself as a Texas cardsharp, Henry turned into "Austin" Antrim for a bit. That nickname didn't stick.

"Shortly after the Kid came to Fort Grant, Windy started abusing him," said cowboy Gus Gildea. "He would throw Billy to the floor, ruffle his hair, slap his face and humiliate him before the men in the saloon. Yes, the Kid was rather slender. . . . The black-smith was a large man with a gruff voice and blustering manner."[3]

By November 1875, the fourteen-year-old Kid settled into an occupation suiting his physical abilities and appealing to his sense of risk taking—horse stealing. In those days, stealing a man's horse was worse than killing him. Many a horse thief found himself "decorating a cottonwood," a common term meaning to hang someone.

Several saloons, dance halls, and a flourishing red-light district sat just outside of Camp Grant's border. "There were many noted bad men drifting in and out. Billy . . . was a young, light, green-looking fellow," reported a construction worker.[4]

"He got to running with a gang of rustlers," wrote Miles L. Wood, the Hotel de Luna owner. Camp Grant's outlying area was the perfect rustlers' gang headquarters where horse thieves could easily steal army mounts.

The Kid fell in with Scottish-born ex-soldier John Mackie (or McKay or McAckey), a twenty-eight-year-old trumpet player recently discharged from the U.S. Army. Similar in size to Mackie, the Kid may have felt a kinship with someone who spoke in an accent reminiscent of his mother's.

He and Mackie stole horses, saddles, and saddle blankets off and on for a year. On November 17, 1876, the fifteen-year-old Kid rode off on a sergeant's horse. Major Compton ordered five troopers to go after him. Five days later and 100 miles away, the men caught up to the Kid. Without a proper arrest warrant and after ordering their quarry off the horse, the troopers grabbed the reins and headed back to camp, leaving the Kid afoot.

Three more horses were stolen three months later. Often, when cavalry troopers were inside a saloon, they would tie ropes to their horses and keep them in hand while drinking or playing cards. A couple of times, the soldiers walked out, rope in hand, only to find the other end tied to the hitch rail and their horses vanished. Enough was enough.

Major Compton was determined to see the Kid behind bars. The newly elected justice of the peace, Miles Wood, the Kid's former employer, signed a warrant against the Kid. He was arrested in Globe City in the Pinal Mountain foothills, but the Kid promptly escaped. The Kid was arrested again the next day and managed to escape once more.

"MORE FRIENDS THAN ENEMIES"

In an effort to "go straight," the Kid and Mackie returned five stolen horses to nearby Camp Thomas. However, the Kid was still a wanted man. When the two men showed up for breakfast at the Hotel de Luna at Camp Grant, Justice Wood waited on them himself, concealing a loaded pistol under the serving tray. The Kid and Mackie gave up immediately.

With no jail in the civilian settlement, Wood and another man had to march the prisoners to the post guardhouse. An hour later, Kid tried to get away, but he didn't get far. This time, Wood asked the blacksmith, Windy Cahill, to place shackles on the Kid's ankles and pound the rivets flat. Certain the young man would stay put, the major relaxed.

He shouldn't have. The post guardhouse, built of overlapping boards, stood upright in a stone foundation and mud mortar. It had a dirt floor, a wood shingle roof, and walls twelve feet high. Along the top ran a narrow ventilation ridge that the sagging roof had conveniently widened. So Mackie boosted the Kid up the wall, where he squeezed through the opening and dropped to the ground. The Kid followed the creek bed out of the post, past the Hotel de Luna, and down to Atkin's cantina, where bartender "Adobe" Tom Varley, who must have been friends with him, pried open the shackles.[5]

That same evening while hosting a party, Major Compton was informed that the Kid was gone. Enraged, the major was certain the Kid had had help escaping and demanded answers. Justice Wood explained the next day that the Kid "was a small fellow not weighing over ninety pounds, and it was almost an impossibility to keep him imprisoned or hand-cuffed."[6]

This would be the first of many times the Kid chose to stay in the area instead of hightailing it for Mexico or California, somewhere safe. Why? Camp Grant cowpuncher Gus Gildea remembered, "Billy always had more friends than enemies." That would prove true over the next four years.

The Kid's personality combined good humor with a flaming, hair-trigger temper. Boldness verged on recklessness, and when provoked, he could explode into deadly rage that carried no warning. However, he was sunny by nature, open, and generous. He laughed frequently, and his smile made him well liked by almost everyone. He boasted a quick mind and superior intelligence, and he could read and write.

The Kid continued to lead the existence of a saddle tramp, a nomadic cowboy, along the New Mexico–Arizona border. He worked at the Gila Ranch for a bit. His closest friends were the *vaqueros* and farmers who taught him how to rope and ride well and how to protect himself with firearms. He also honed his Spanish skills. He learned well, becoming an excellent horseman, learning how to break *mesteños* (mustangs), and easily grasping cowboy lingo. Sometime during this period, he became acquainted with a group of rustlers known as the "Boys" led by Jesse J. Evans.

NO LONGER AN ANTRIM
Through the fall of 1876 and spring of 1877, the Kid had his choice of twelve saloons in which to play poker and deal monte. More than likely, he tended bar at Isaac's Saloon as Austin Antrim. It was here, during an indoor shooting competition, that the Kid took aim at John Brannaman but hit Phineas Clanton (one of the Ike Clanton clan) in the mouth, taking his two front teeth. As one newspaper commented, "Such is life in new mining camps."[7]

Around this time, Bill Antrim became aware of his stepson's new profession and widened the distance between himself and the Kid. He returned to Silver City in February 1877 and refused to claim any relation to the Kid. With the last tendril of a family pulled out from under him on learning of this rebuff, angry, hurt, and betrayed, the Kid erased his stepfather from memory and took on yet another name: Billy Bonney (Bonney was his brother's middle name). Later, in a letter to New Mexico Territory Governor Lew Wallace, Billy stated, "Antrim is my stepfather's name."

By the summer of 1877, sixteen-year-old Billy had grown physically. "Slim, muscular, wiry, and erect, weighing 135 pounds and standing five-feet-seven-inches tall, he was lithe and vigorous in his movements. Wavy brown hair topped an oval face betraying the down of incipient mustache and beard. Expressive blue eyes caught everyone's notice. So did two slightly protruding front teeth. They were especially visible when he smiled or laughed, which was nearly always, but people found them pleasing."[8]

Keeping himself neat, the Kid wore simple, useful clothing—black frock coat, dark pants and vest, and boots. His most conspicuous garb was a simple Mexican sombrero that protected him from the harsh southwestern sun.

HIS FIRST KILLING

The Kid went to work at a hay camp owned by "Sorghum" Smith, an army contractor. Smith said this about the Kid: "He said he was seventeen, though he didn't look to be fourteen. I gave him a job helping around camp. He hadn't worked very long until he wanted his money. I asked him if he was going to quit. He said, 'No, I want to buy some things.' I asked how much he wanted and tried to get him to take $10 . . . but he hesitated and asked for $40. I gave it to him. He went down to the post trader and bought himself a whole outfit: six shooter, belt, scabbard, and cartridges."[9]

Always one to take pride in what he wore, the Kid showed up at George Atkin's cantina on Friday, August 17, 1877. Gus Gildea saw him come "to town dressed like a 'country jake,' with 'store pants' on and shoes instead of boots."[10] He had a six-gun stuck in the waistband of his trousers since he couldn't afford a holster. The Kid must have felt like a new man.

The easygoing, likable teenager got into an argument with his adversary Windy Cahill. True to form, the blacksmith began harassing the Kid. Cahill called him a pimp—true fighting words in those days. Kid returned the favor by calling Cahill a son of a bitch. Understandably, a fight erupted just as Justice Wood walked in. Kid and Cahill got to wrestling to see who could throw the other first. Cahill, larger and stouter than the Kid, threw him three times. Kid's anger seethed. Cahill then pinned his arms down with his knees and started slapping his face.

"You're hurting me. Let me up!" hollered the Kid.

"I want to hurt you. That's why I got you down."

People in the saloon gave them plenty of space.

Pushed to the brink, the Kid's lightning-fast temper boiled to the surface. "Billy's right arm was free from the elbow down. He started working his hand around and finally managed to grasp his forty-five. . . . The blacksmith evidently felt the pistol against his side, for he straightened slightly. Then there was a deafening roar. Windy slumped to the side as the Kid squirmed free," stated witness Gildea.

As Justice Wood saw it, the Kid "pulled his six gun and stuck it in the stomach and fired and killed Cahill."[11]

The Kid rushed out of the saloon, jumped on the nearest horse, Cashaw, said to be the fastest horse in the valley, and galloped east.

Justice Wood convened an inquest in the Hotel de Luna, where all the jurors decided that "the shooting was criminal and unjustifiable, and Henry Antrim alias Kid, is guilty thereof."

Not everyone agreed, thinking Cahill got what he deserved, seeing the Kid's act as one of self-defense. Gus Gildea argued, "He had no choice. He had to use his 'equalizer.'"

Although the courts took his crime seriously, there is no doubt that if the Kid had stayed to face his accusers, he would have been found not guilty. With all the witnesses around, some Kid fans and some not, the truth would have emerged. The Code of the West, which stated you can kill in self-defense, was in force and regularly used in courtrooms.

Unfortunately, the Kid wasn't willing to take any chances. He fled Arizona, rushing back to the only place he might be safe: New Mexico. Either way, the Kid's life took a perilous turn when Windy Cahill gasped his last breath.

CHAPTER SEVEN

OUTLAW DAYS: THE KID RETURNS

"He was indeed a kid who had been left rudderless after his mother's death . . . he was frequently impetuous and made errors in judgement."

—MICHAEL WALLIS, AUTHOR OF
THE ENDLESS RIDE OF BILLY THE KID

CONVINCED A POSSE WAS ON HIS HEELS, THE ONLY PLACE THE Kid knew to go after galloping out of Arizona was back to Silver City—maybe not the best choice considering he thought he was still a wanted man. But even the Kid realized that killing a man held more dire consequences than simply stealing laundry. It had been two years since his questionable association with bad characters like Sombrero Jack. Surely, the law, Sheriff Whitehill in particular, had forgotten—or forgiven—by now.

Although he "fled the scene," which might at first blush seem a cowardly thing to do, his dustup with Cahill shows the Kid's true nature and the kind of man he was becoming. He stood his ground, even against an oversized bully—and won. He held his own. Reports that he was a scrawny runt fail to mention that while he was slender, he was also wiry, lean, and muscled. Some friends mentioned he was lithe as a cat, especially on the dance floor. But he was no lightweight when it came to fending for himself or fending off bullies. He had stood up to Cahill but hadn't meant to kill him. The Kid knew what he'd done was wrong, and he also thought he wouldn't get a fair trial. His sense of honor and morals, most likely instilled by Catherine, gave him reason to flee Arizona.

So he rode east. By the first week in September, he had taken refuge at the Richard Knight ranch in the Burro Mountains, forty miles south of Silver City. The Kid's friend Tony Conner, Mrs. Knight's brother, remembered his arrival. "He told the folks what he had done. He remained there about two weeks but fearing the officers from Arizona might show up almost any time, he left for Lincoln County and never returned."[1]

A week after arriving at Knight's ranch, he asked a man traveling through to Arizona if he would take Cashaw, the racing pony he'd "borrowed" during his frantic escape from Arizona, and return the horse to its rightful owner, John Murphey. The man did.

Understandably, the Kid was fearful. No doubt in his mind, a posse was moments away from either arresting him or shooting him. What he didn't know was that law enforcement was stretched thin and that only the most chronic and heinous criminals were pursued. Lawmen were busy with marauding Indians as well as a flood of men from the East who were truly hardened criminals. Men who had fought in the Civil War and had killed, robbed, and raped came west looking for more of the same. The Kid's crimes paled in comparison. The Arizona authorities would have done nothing to search for a fugitive who had vanished, especially for a crime in which the killing had been declared self-defense by many eyewitnesses. Although the Kid's crimes were inconsequential to both Arizona and New Mexico authorities, they were *not* inconsequential to him. He looked over his shoulder constantly.

A FINAL GOOD-BYE

The Kid left Knight's ranch, skirted Silver City, and drifted to Ed Moulton's sawmill. No longer friendly once he heard about the

Kid's escapades, Moulton recommended he leave soon and get as far away as possible. The Kid took the hint and managed to find his former teacher, Mary Richards, in Georgetown. She had married and retired from teaching, as was customary at the time. Only single women worked as teachers. They spent a few hours talking, and then he mounted up and rode off.

Perhaps realizing he was careening down the wrong path, the Kid sought to close the chapter on one portion of his life. In late September 1877, he went looking for his brother. The Kid found Josie (now Joseph) living with Chauncey Truesdell on a ranch north of Georgetown. The brothers spent hours sharing stories. Finally, after wishing each other well, they hugged and shook hands for the last time. They would never see each other again.

ONE OF THE "BOYS"

The Silver City and La Mesilla newspapers reported on the multi-faceted conflict in Lincoln County between two factions competing for profits from dry goods and cattle interests. The simmering pot of greed and corruption would explode in 1878. They also wrote about the shooting of Windy Cahill. Critical of the lawlessness, *Mesilla Valley Independent* editor Albert J. Fountain dubbed the organized crime running rampant throughout the lower half of New Mexico the "Banditti." The articles alerted citizens to the ongoing activities of the "Banditti of New Mexico." With each robbery, the gang became more emboldened. They even threatened John Chisum's cattle drives from Lincoln into Arizona.

Employed by Chisum's competitors and led by his former drovers Jesse Evans and Frank Baker, the Banditti were reportedly cutting out cattle on the fringes of moving herds, claiming to have resold them at $10 a head. A tidy profit.

Being well read, the Kid would have read about the mayhem rampaging over the territory. When sawmill owner Ed Moulton asked the Kid which side he would be on, the Kid replied he wasn't sure. That didn't last long.

While the Kid was brave, fortified with nerves of steel and a moral compass, he often put his trust in the hands of the wrong friends. On the road between Silver City and La Mesilla, he stopped for the night at Apache Tejo, a settlement and watering stop on the ruins of Old Fort McLane, south of Silver City. The Kid kept one eye open for sheriffs and a posse. What he spotted was a wild group of men galloping into the area, a string of unsaddled horses and mules tugging at their reins. It was the Banditti returning from a horse-stealing raid in Lincoln.

Undoubtedly, the Kid stood stunned at the spectacle. What he didn't know was that he'd just met the Boys, a bunch of hard-riding thieves and rustlers, part of an outlaw network led by rancher John Kinney of La Mesilla. This band of the Boys was led by Jesse Evans, a former cowboy for cattleman John Chisum. The group was made up of ex-soldiers, rogue cowboys, and *pistoleros*, Mexicans, Americans, and Indians who brazenly stole horses and cattle. They also killed anyone in their way. Surely, there was safety in numbers, and this was a group in which the Kid could hide out. He knew all about stealing horses.

The Boys offered employment (sort of) and appeared to operate ignored by the law—exactly what he needed. The Kid, now calling himself Kid Antrim, joined them.

Kid's Silver City friend Louis Abraham said, "Billy had no reason, only fear, for he hung around Apache Tejo for quite a while, and Sheriff Whitehill could have gotten him if he had wanted him punished."[2] But as long as Kid Antrim rode with the Boys, their fellowship was a near guarantee that he would not get caught. He blended in well with the other men.

While they headquartered at Apache Tejo, the brains behind the gang, John Kinney, provided a rendezvous point in La Mesilla for all his various bands of outlaws. Kinney was the one who planned the forays and called the shots of who went where. As soon as the Boys brought a herd of stolen horses or cattle to him, Kinney would then sell the stock to ranchers and butchers who weren't too picky about brands and bills of sale.

The Kid had learned a great deal during his two years in Arizona. His association with rough-and-tough cowboys and rustlers initiated him into a lawless culture that stressed every man must ride and shoot well.

"When he fled the New Mexico Territory as a petty thief, he was a fifteen-year-old boy, but during the time he spent in Arizona, the Kid had come of age. Reputation on the outlaw level traveled fast, and the fact that the Kid had killed a man was a mark in his favor."[3]

According to several of Kid's acquaintances, he was affable and gregarious, loved a good joke, and possessed plenty of charisma. His mind was agile, and although he didn't use tobacco and rarely drank, he enjoyed the company of men and women in the saloons and cantinas. He took pleasure in the dances and *bailes*, just as he had with his mother. All it took was a flash of his charming personality and a smile, and women flocked to him. Since he spoke Spanish fluently, he was always welcomed.

On October 1, 1877, Kid Antrim and nine other outlaws swooped down on the L. F. Pass coal camp in the Burro Mountains, sixteen miles southwest of Silver City, the Kid's old stomping grounds. They stole three horses and lit out south for La Mesilla. Along the way, a Silver City resident encountered the outlaws and recognized Kid in the mix. Area newspapers soon reported the sighting.

"Sometime on Tuesday, the party of thieves, among whom was Henry Antrim, were met in Cook's [sic] canon [sic] by Mr. Carpenter."[4]

Stealing horses wasn't enough. On their way down to La Mesilla, they chanced on a stagecoach making its way west. The Boys demanded money since most stages carried passengers, mail, and payroll. However, on this particular run, the driver assured them he had no money and carried no bullion or anything of value other than his life. They reluctantly let him continue but only after he took a pull from a bottle with the gang. The driver later told a newspaper reporter that there were nine men in the gang, including Jesse Evans.

A few days later, the Kid was riding with twenty-six boys as heavily armed members showed up with more stolen horses. This gave the Boys enough firepower to force a large posse carrying only pistols into a canyon while waiting for reinforcements. Intent on delivering their stolen herd of horses, the gang rode off, jeering at the posse.

In October 1877, the Boys stopped for provisions at a trading post near the Mescalero Apache Indian Agency, then made their way to the summit of the Sacramento Mountains. There, they met up with John Riley, partner of the Murphy-Dolan mercantile firm. A riotous evening passed—and rightly so since the Boys provided stolen cattle to James J. Dolan (later of Lincoln County War fame), who then sold them to the army and reservation Apache. As a group, they were unknowingly heading straight into what would become the infamous Lincoln County War.

During the fall of 1877, the gang grew more and more violent, stealing greater quantities of cattle, horses, and money. One of the Boys, a man named "Fence Rail," and newspaper editor Albert Fountain participated in a war of words published in the *Mesilla Valley Independent*. Fountain condemned organized crime in his editorials, and "Fence Rail" wrote these chilling words: "That the public is our oyster, and that having the power, we claim the right to appropriate any property we may take a fancy to, and that we exercise that right regardless of consequences."[5]

ME? NO LONGER ONE OF THE BOYS

Although Kid Antrim had ridden with the Boys for about six weeks, he failed to become one of them. He didn't think like they did and found fault with their move toward greater violence. It must have been a challenge for the small Kid to hold his own against these hardened criminals, most of them physically bigger than he. But again, he'd grown from a boy into a man who would stand his own ground.

Somewhere around La Mesilla, the Kid split with the gang, who headed up the west side of the Sacramento Mountains. At that time, the Kid was still going with the last name Antrim when he reached Dona Ana County and La Mesilla in southern New Mexico. The Kid looked for work at a ranch owned by Eugene Van Patten, but it's unclear if the rancher hired him. In La Mesilla, the Kid met Tom O'Keefe, a young man his age, and they hit it off. Tom was headed to the Pecos Valley in search of work, so the Kid went too.

They rode together through the spiked Organ Mountains east of La Mesilla, through San Augustin Pass, and then across the vast desert of the Tularosa Basin. Instead of taking a safer route through the Tularosa, Ruidoso, and Hondo valleys, the boys took a shortcut straight over the northern part of the Guadalupe Mountains. Either they didn't know or they ignored the fact that most travelers on this trail fell victim to roving bands of renegade Apache.

On the second day of their adventure, the Kid spotted a pool of water at the bottom of the canyon below. With empty canteens in hand, he left Tom and the horses waiting on the trail while he climbed down to the pool. Enjoying a splash of cool water on his face, he then filled the canteens and turned around for the return climb.

Gunfire pierced the quiet. Taking cover behind rocks and brush, the Kid scrambled back up the hill only to discover the horses gone. Tom was gone. His bedroll and supplies were gone. At least he had a canteen.

He walked east. For three days, he trudged through the Guadalupes, sleeping days and walking nights, before coming on the Heiskell Jones Ranch. Footsore and near death, the Kid nearly collapsed into a woman's arms. Heiskell's wife, Barbara Culp Jones, had found him outside. Everyone called her "Ma'am Jones," and she doctored his blistered feet and fed him for a couple of weeks.

He introduced himself as Billy Bonney. This was the first time he'd been known to use that alias.

The Jones family, which included nine sons and one daughter, became deeply attached to Billy. In an interview years later, Ma'am Jones maintained she was the first person to encounter Kid Antrim in Lincoln County. She recollected that in the pre-dawn darkness, she heard rustling in the mesquite outside the cabin. With her husband away on business, she was the one to defend her brood. She reached for her Winchester and peered through a slit in the wall.

"A slender boy arose and stumbled unsteadily toward the house," Ma'am Jones said. "He dropped the rifle, and I ran to meet the boy . . . half carried him to the kitchen . . . he pulled off one boot . . . he wore no socks, and his feet were raw and swollen."[6]

While Billy was resting and practicing his gun skills at the Joneses' ranch, a determined posse led by Dick Brewer, deputized foreman of the Lincoln County grand jury and foreman for rancher/business owner John Tunstall, tracked the Boys to a dugout near the Beckwith Ranch outside of Lincoln. The posse surrounded the spread.

At dawn, shots were fired. Many shots. No one was hit. Jesse Evans later said he couldn't figure out how he missed Brewer, as "he had three fair, square shots at him, and he was saving his shots for him alone. The bullets struck within four or five inches of him each time."[7]

When a standoff ensued, the posse yelled at the outlaws that if they surrendered, they would not be lynched. Jesse Evans, his first lieutenant Frank Baker, and two others came out, hands up. The four outlaws were taken to the only "jail," a muddy dugout in Lincoln.

Meanwhile, a few miles away at the Joneses' ranch, Billy enjoyed more of Ma'am Jones's cooking. But enjoying time with a family and eating good cooking would soon come to an end.

CHAPTER EIGHT

TRIED TO GO STRAIGHT

"In frontier New Mexico, life was cheap and killing was not considered a particularly heinous crime."
—WARREN BECK, HISTORIAN

BILLY BONNEY STAYED ON AT THE JONESES' RANCH FOR MORE than two weeks. Although he did chores to help out, he mostly practiced shooting with John Jones (the oldest of the nine boys). Those days must have been glorious. He met George and Frank Coe, cousins who ranched nearby. The three would become lifelong friends. Both Coes were fiddlers, meaning Billy tagged along whenever they played at the dances. Billy danced and sang (and broke señoritas' hearts) all night until the sun wormed its way into the barns.

In a later interview, George Coe recalled, "Billy lost no time getting to know the other people in the valley. He was the center of attention everywhere he went, and though heavily armed, he seemed as gentlemanly as a college-bred youth. He quickly became acquainted with everybody, and because of his humorous and pleasing personality grew to be a community favorite.

"In fact, Billy was so popular there wasn't enough of him to go around. He had a beautiful voice and sang like a bird. One of our special amusements was to get together every few nights and have a singing. The thrill of those happy nights still lingers."[1]

A widow and her children were also staying at the Joneses' ranch while Billy recovered his strength. The fourteen-year-old daughter was clearly smitten with Billy when she wrote, "The Kid was active and graceful as a cat. At Seven Rivers he practiced continually with pistol or rifle, riding at a run and dodging behind the side of his mount to fire, as the Apaches did. He was very proud of his ability to pick up a handkerchief or other object from the ground while riding at a run."

Her brother wasn't quite as entranced. "When I knowed him at Seven Rivers, you might call him a bum. He was nothing but a kid and a bum."[2]

"I found Billy different from most boys of his age," Frank Coe said in an interview many years later. "He had been thrown on his own resources from early boyhood. From his own statement to me, he hadn't known what it meant to be a boy; at the age of twelve he was associated with men of twenty-five and older. Billy was eager to learn everything and had a most active and fertile mind."[3]

The Joneses' ranch was situated near the village of Seven Rivers on the Pecos. Seven Rivers, named after the springs feeding into the river, was a good resting place for the many cattle drives passing through the Pecos River valley.

Although a favorite gathering spot for ranchers and drovers, it also had a reputation as a hangout for cattle rustlers, rowdies, and gamblers. According to local legend, there were so many shootings in town that all the saloon doors had removable hinges so they could be easily used as stretchers for the wounded.

Determined to straighten out his life, Billy took a deep breath and considered alternatives. He was good with horses and great with guns. Wanting to make honest wages and distance himself further from the Boys, Billy read about rancher John Chisum near Lincoln paying $3 a day for ranch hands. It was hard to resist that

Charles Bowdre arrived in Lincoln County in 1874 and opened a cheese factory on the Gila River with friend Doc Scurlock. Bowdre was killed at Stinking Springs, and this *carte de visite*, taken off his body by Sheriff Garrett, shows his blood drops on it.

kind of money and, it was hoped, stability. Billy set his sights on Lincoln.

If Billy was going to succeed in Lincoln, especially as a ranch hand or cowboy, the Joneses' knew he would need a horse, so they gave him one. He met rancher Charles Bowdre, who would become a close friend, and went to work for him. Being able to read and write was a plus, and he did both well. Being bilingual also put him in good stead with the ranchers and local Hispanics. A hard worker but still small in stature, Billy finally understood and accepted his limitations. He could herd cattle with the best of them from the back of a horse, but being a ranch hand and throwing 100-pound hay bales as they did was out of his reach.

STORM CLOUDS OVER LINCOLN

The sparsely populated New Mexico Territory accounted for 15 percent of all murders *in the nation*, and by 1880, the homicide rate was forty-seven times higher than the national average. Much of the violence occurred in Lincoln County. The village of Lincoln was the center of one of the most lawless areas of the entire country. At least fifty people died in the 1870s along the one-mile stretch of dusty road curving through Bonita Valley and Lincoln. Violence was so bad that in 1878, President Rutherford B. Hayes declared Lincoln the "Most Dangerous Street in America."

Except for the Native Americans who had lived in the region for generations, most everyone in Lincoln was new to the territory, many of them Irish immigrants. In the 1850s and early 1860s, Mexicans and Hispanics established ranches and farmed the fertile area near the many streams. Texas cattlemen, like John Chisum, extended their ranches and herds into New Mexico and Arizona.

Lincoln County was established by an act of the territorial legislature in 1869. General William Tecumseh Sherman, on tour for the War Department in 1874, raised an eyebrow and said the territory was "not worth the cost of defense." Apparently, that feeling was shared by many, especially those on the East Coast. By 1878, Lincoln County comprised 27,000 square miles, or 20 million acres, which was one-fourth of the state, making it the largest county in the nation. North to south, it measured 170 miles, east to west 150 miles. Like a double-edged sword, Lincoln was far away from the larger, more power-wielding towns of Santa Fe, Albuquerque, and La Mesilla—good news if you were dodging the law, bad news if you were an honest citizen trying to keep from being shot or having your cattle stolen. The "law" was too far away to do much good.

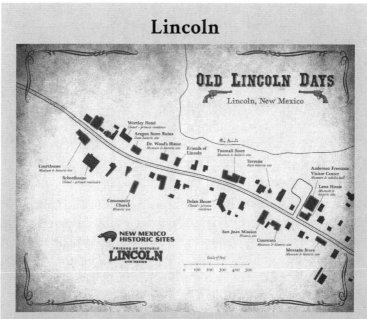

Lincoln today hasn't changed much since Billy's days. Unlike many villages, Lincoln has one street, which is also highway U.S. 380. Visitors can enjoy walking through history here.

MAP PRODUCED BY OLD WEST MAPS AND COURTESY OF NEW MEXICO HISTORIC SITES AND FRIENDS OF HISTORIC LINCOLN

Set in the narrow Bonito Valley between the Sacramento and Capitan mountains rising on both sides, Lincoln in the 1860s was one street. Today, it is still one street. The Rio Bonito, clear and cold, cuts through the valley, providing water for irrigation, cattle, and people. The area, usually cold and snowy in winter and then remaining cool for many months, doesn't allow for much farming. Gardens are few, but onions grow well, as do potatoes in other parts of the county. Salt, which is found aboveground, is shoveled.

Mail in Billy's time arrived on buckboard from Las Vegas, New Mexico, by way of Fort Sumner and Roswell. Approximately half of the village residents were either Irish immigrants or, like Billy, Irish descendants. The other half were Hispanic, many families having lived in the area for generations, or Mexicans who traveled north for better grazing and to establish ranches.

Originally called La Placita del Rio Bonito (The Place by the Pretty River) by the Mexican families who settled it in the 1850s, the name of the community was changed to Lincoln when Lincoln County was created on January 16, 1869.

LINCOLN COUNTY WAR'S MAJOR PLAYERS: MURPHY-DOLAN FACTION

Into Lincoln stepped Irish immigrant Lawrence Murphy, who had served in the army under Kit Carson in the 1860s. He had been instrumental in moving the Navajos to the Bosque Redondo at Fort Stanton on their "Long Walk" and quelling the Mescalero Apaches. Once he became a civilian, he and fellow army veteran Emil Fritz established L. G. Murphy & Co. at the fort, operating as a post trader. His company contracted to supply beef, corn, and other foodstuffs to soldiers. He quickly had a stranglehold on the economy, becoming the "mercantile axis of Lincoln County."[4]

Murphy and Fritz built a store and brewery at the fort and also in Lincoln. Business boomed until Murphy's bookkeeper, quick-tempered Irishman James Dolan, threatened to shoot Fort

Constructed in 1873–1874, the only two-story building in town (known as the Big House) held a store downstairs and living quarters upstairs. Pictured are Sheriff James Brent (sixth from left) with his deputies, ca. 1886. This is the earliest known photograph of the Lincoln County Courthouse.
AUTHOR'S COLLECTION

Stanton's captain. Dolan's continued verbal outbursts and threats got Murphy's company booted from the fort in 1870. Murphy moved his headquarters to Lincoln, where, in 1873–1874, he erected an imposing two-story store and residence—the largest in the county—costing him $7,000. This building would later become the courthouse and jail.

Around 1874, Murphy took James Dolan on as a junior partner. Like Murphy, Dolan was an Irish immigrant and army veteran. Known as a hothead, he was small boned and short (five feet, three inches tall), belligerent, but hardworking. And for some reason, he and Murphy hit it off well.

They ran the county, picking up most of the beef contracts with the army forts and Indian agencies—quite lucrative in all regards. Naturally, competition was not tolerated.

Murphy's health was not the best, so Dolan increasingly became the company's face. In fact, he threw himself into community affairs, burning down a ranch but also becoming the Lincoln postmaster. In 1874, Murphy, suffering from alcoholism and cancer, willed the company to Dolan, probably not the best choice of successors since short-tempered Dolan would go on to kill a man on May 9, 1877. Dolan claimed it was self-defense, but he continued to grow more erratic, more violent.

Into the mix came twenty-four-year-old Englishman John Tunstall, who arrived in Lincoln in October 1876. Tunstall had left his father's mercantile business in Vancouver, British Columbia, and moved into Lincoln County to start a ranch. In addition to buying mules, horses, harnesses, saddles, and so on, he also opened a bank and a general mercantile store. Some say he was arrogant, asthmatic, and blind in one eye.

Tunstall, unlike so many other Englishmen who came to the West, was not prompted by any desire to squander his inherited wealth. Neither careless nor adventurous, he tended to be soft spoken and not quarrelsome, attending strictly to his own business. Tunstall was raised in an English home full of culture and refinement, and he

The first man killed in the Lincoln County War was Englishman John Tunstall, who in 1876 drove his herd of cattle to the Felix Valley and occupied a dugout until he could build a four-room adobe house at the upper springs of the Felix River. The dugout was then used as a rider's camp for his men. It is believed that Billy the Kid stayed there while working for him.

AUTHOR'S COLLECTION

believed religiously in the rights of others, wanting nothing but what rightfully belonged to him. Prompt in paying his bills, a lesson he learned from his father back in England, he did not run into debt, nor did he owe money during his business career in Lincoln.

In 1875, Alexander McSween, an attorney from the Midwest, and his wife Susan arrived in Lincoln. He first met Murphy and Dolan but shied away from their schemes. When Tunstall, who decided to open a bank and provide beef to the army, arrived in November 1876, McSween knew there was something about the man he liked. Soon, he and rancher John Chisum chose to fall in with Tunstall. The Tunstall-McSween-Chisum faction competed head-on with Murphy-Dolan-Riley. To Tunstall's way of thinking, in order to break the business monopoly of the "House" (the local nickname for Murphy-Dolan enterprises), he would establish a competing store and bank.

A war for political power and economic control of Lincoln County threatened to explode when Murphy and his partners questioned McSween, accusing him of misusing

Alexander McSween played a pivotal role in the Lincoln County War, first working for Murphy-Dolan, then partnering with John Tunstall. AUTHOR'S COLLECTION

money from an insurance policy. At the same time, while Chisum and McSween were organizing a bank, Tunstall was buying a ranch east of Lincoln.

Billy may have met and possibly even worked for cattleman John Chisum in Arizona. Tennessee-born "Cattle King" Chisum ran his ever-expanding herds from eastern New Mexico to the forts in Arizona. He employed more than 100 hands, some of whom, such as Jesse Evans, were not above culling a few of the slower beeves to sell for a tidy personal profit.

The moniker "Cattle King" fit him perfectly, as his range of low-rolling, highly grassed spread covered more than fifty miles up and down the Pecos River north of Seven Rivers. Here, he ran between 60,000 and 80,000 head of full-blooded, graded Texas cattle. Each one sported Chisum's Long Rail brand and distinctive Jinglebob earmark.

Others claim, however, that Chisum didn't exactly buy the rich, grazing land his cattle enjoyed (more like he "squatted" on the acreage). He didn't appear bothered that he was pushing out established Hispanic farmers who'd worked since the mid-1800s to build successful ranches. He tended to take what he needed.

Butting heads with Murphy & Co., Chisum furnished beef to the government for the Indian reservations and army posts in New Mexico, Arizona, and West Texas. Such a deal was highly desirable because they paid cash on delivery. Understandably, competition among the cattlemen was intense.

The "Ring"

Men who would figure prominently in Billy's fate were District Attorney William Rynerson, Sheriff James Brady, Judge Warren Bristol, and several local authorities, all in Murphy-Dolan pockets. If that wasn't enough, the House was backed by the "Santa Fe Ring," a corrupt conglomeration of crooked state politicians, businessmen, land swindlers, cattle thieves, judges, and lawyers. "Their cronies included hired gunmen and tainted lawmen that used the law to suit themselves. They held sway in New Mexico from the 1870s until around 1900."[5]

Chief among the Ring were Thomas B. Catron, a shrewd lawyer instrumental in stealing more than 80 percent of the Spanish land grants of New Mexico; Lucien B. Maxwell, an "entrepreneur" and one of the men who acquired the almost 2-million-acre Maxwell Land Grant, which covered several entire Hispanic villages and grants; and John Chisum, who preempted public grazing lands for his herd of cattle.[6] Essentially, the Ring controlled the whole of New Mexico Territory because Governor Lew Wallace provided these men leeway.

At the center of the "feud" stood the fact that half of Lincoln was Irish immigrants who hated and feared the English who had run them out of their homeland. Irish natives Murphy and Dolan fueled that fire every time they ran into Tunstall. No wonder tension in town was palpable.

Sixteen-year-old Billy Bonney entered the scene when he signed on to work with Tunstall in late 1877. At that time, Lincoln was a thriving community with a church, businesses, a history of Apache raids, as well as men and women looking to reinvent themselves after the tragedies of the Civil War. Anti-Chisum sentiment rumbled across the plain, and when Billy rode into town, he stepped into a muddy quagmire of stinking political maneuverings. It was the wild-and-woolly West at its worst and best.

When Billy met John Tunstall, Billy was already distinguished for his prowess with a gun and his magnetic personality. His contemporaries stated to a man that he "was a gentleman with the ladies, had a high regard for motherhood and the elderly, had a cheerful disposition and good nature, and was a very likeable fellow."[7]

Billy's friend Frank Coe told the *El Paso Times* in a 1923 interview, "The Kid, however, was by far the quickest with a pistol; he could empty all six chambers of a revolver while an ordinary man was firing his first shot. He never seemed to take aim but appeared to have an instinctive control."[8]

In his own words, Billy explained to John Jones that although he was ambidextrous and could write well with his left, he was not as good a shooter with that hand. "Sometimes I hit, but if I was in a jackpot, I'd use my right."[9]

Tunstall took the teenager under his wing. More than likely, the British accent reminded Billy of his ma, and the man's values may have been something Billy admired. Working for Tunstall gave Billy the sense of belonging and security he'd been searching for. He dreamed of his future, planning with friend Fred Waite to pool their money and buy a small ranch, to settle down.

Certainly, by this time, Billy knew of the storm clouds gathering over the small town of Lincoln. He read the newspapers and listened to conversations. Little did Billy know that within a few months, he would be the central figure in the deadliest clash Lincoln County had ever seen. Moreover, with all the Irish brogues and Irish customs around him, he must have felt right at home.

While political maneuvering was taking place, Billy enjoyed staying in San Patricio, a small village on the Rio Ruidoso, slightly above the junction with the Rio Bonito. Originally called Ruidoso, the name was changed in 1875 when a church named San Patricio, the patron saint of Ireland, was built and supervised by an Irish priest. Here, the Irish and Hispanic population embraced Billy while he embraced the señoritas. Dick Brewer, Tunstall ranch foreman, said in a 1938 interview, "Billy had more sweethearts on the creek than a little."[10]

The Many Loves of Billy the Kid

We've all heard about a sailor with a woman in every port. Billy had a woman in every town. All we can do is list women who've been romantically attached to Billy. Whether his personal charisma was as alluring as reported, it seemed he courted the entire eastern side of the New Mexico Territory.

Abrana Garcia

Descendants of Abrana claim she was a Navajo captured as a child and raised by Utes and then freed. At twenty-two, she was married with three children, two by her husband of a previous marriage. In 1880, she had a five-month-old. A long-held oral tradition among her family says she was indeed Billy's girlfriend and had a son by him.

Sallie Chisum

For a while, eighteen-year-old Sallie Chisum was one of Billy's favorite *novias*. Niece of rancher John Chisum, she met Billy at the Chisum Ranch, where her father James and his brother Pitzer worked. There at the ranch, winsome Sallie and teenaged Billy rode horses together across the scrub-dotted rolling hills and wide-sweeping plains of southeastern New Mexico.

They also enjoyed spending late afternoon hours sitting on the porch sharing stories. She wrote in her diary that Billy had given her an Indian tobacco sack and some candy hearts.

Celsa Gutierrez

Much has been written and speculated about Celsa Gutierrez. Unfortunately, there were two Celsa Gutierrezes, both twenty-three, in Lincoln for the 1880 census. Some historians believe one of the Celsas was Billy's paramour; others say no. But if one could guess, Billy's *novia* would be Celsa, whose sister, Juanita, was married for a few days to Pat Garrett, who was serving as deputy sheriff of Lincoln County. Not surprisingly in a small, close-knit community, everybody knew everybody's business. It was no surprise that Billy was smitten with Celsa, a sweet, dark-eyed beauty. Rumors flew about their attraction, although Celsa tried to keep the relationship quiet. Women talked, chitchatting with each other—no secrets in Fort Sumner, especially when Celsa's parents took in a baby boy to raise, Celsa's son, Candido. He reported in later years he knew he was born out of wedlock but didn't know his father's identity. Not much is known about what happened to Celsa after Billy was killed.

Paulita Maxwell

Paulita was rumored to have been Billy's last girlfriend, and she was at Maxwell House the night Billy was murdered. Read more about Paulita in chapter 10.

Nasaria Yerby

Not much is known about Nasaria Yerby, the young "housekeeper" of Thomas Yerby. The 1880 census lists her as unmarried with a three-year-old son and a one-year-old daughter, Florintina. Again, according to the rumor mill of a small town and what the women of the community knew, the little girl was commonly thought to be Billy's child.

And the Others

The other women who surfaced most often were Carlotta Baca (Lincoln), Emily Bruja (Roswell), Lily Huntress (Sunnyside), Minnie Shield (Anton Chico), and Emily Schulander (Las Vegas). There were more, plenty more, but their names have been lost.

Billy worked ten weeks for John Tunstall, who gave him a horse, a Winchester '73 rifle, and a .41 Colt double-action Thunderer, which quickly became his favorite. Tunstall wanted nothing but capable men riding for him, paying them well above the usual salary of $30 a month. Most of all, Tunstall provided stability.

Francisco Gomez, a resident of Lincoln County for seventy-five years, spoke later about Billy's competence. "He used to practice target shooting a lot. He would throw up a can and would twirl his six-gun on his finger and could hit the can six times before it hit the ground." Gomez continued, "He rode a big roan horse about ten or twelve hands high all that winter (1877) and when the horse was out in the pasture, Billy would go to the gate and whistle. That horse would follow Billy around like a dog."[11]

DEATH OF JOHN TUNSTALL

In what became the catalyst for the Lincoln County War, Murphy and his side of the law filed suit against McSween and Tunstall. Judge Warren Bristol issued writs for property and livestock seizures. They took cattle from Tunstall's ranch and goods from the mercantile store in Lincoln.

On February 18, 1878, Billy, Tunstall, and the other hands drove a herd of nine horses that had been exempt from seizure toward Lincoln. At the same time, a posse organized by Sheriff William Brady and led by Jimmy Dolan rode to Tunstall's ranch. Finding only blacksmith Gus Gauss (who would be important to Billy in the future) and another man there, Dolan decided that the nine horses were legally part of the seized animals after all.

A group from Brady's posse, Jesse Evans (the Boys) included, trailed Tunstall. Catching up with them late in the afternoon, they found Tunstall alone with the herd, the other men out looking for wild turkeys.

One of Tunstall's men saw the ambush coming, and he yelled for him to run for cover. Instead, Tunstall approached the posse as if to discuss the issue. As he drew closer, Buck Morton leveled his rifle and shot Tunstall through the upper chest. The Englishman tumbled from his horse. As if that wasn't enough of an insult, posse man Tom Hill dismounted, picked up Tunstall's pistol, and shot him point-blank in the back of the head. Hill then shot and killed Tunstall's prized bay horse.

Then the posse rode off with the horses.

Tunstall's murder pulled the rug out from under Billy's feet once again. The man he considered an older brother was dead, and any sense of security was gone. A shattered Billy turned angry and violent.

"If Tunstall had lived," George Coe said later, "the Kid would have been known as William H. Bonney, a respectable member of society and a valuable citizen. Billy was a brave, resourceful, and honest boy; he would have been a successful man under other circumstances. I loved the youngster in the old days, and can say now, after the passing of fifty years, that I still love his memory."[12]

While news of the murder spread, Tunstall's body was laid on a table in McSween's parlor. Billy, sombrero in hand, came to pay his respects. Frank Coe was there and remembered that the "Kid walked up, looked at Tunstall and said, 'I'll get some of them before I die' and turned away."[13]

CHAPTER NINE

ALL HELL BREAKS LOOSE

"There were many good traits about Billy. . . . He wasn't what you'd call a killer. He never made a gun play he didn't mean, and he never shot up a town. I've met worse men than Billy."

—Sheriff Pat Garrett

To make sure they'd get the control they desired, both opposing factions finally resorted to violence. Murder and the manipulation of governors, lawmen, and judges whose integrity was often questionable served one side well. When a posse allied with Dolan murdered John Tunstall, as they say, "all hell broke loose."

And Billy was ready to lead the revenge charge. While he was usually a likable, lovable, easygoing seventeen-year-old, Tunstall's murder pushed him closer to the edge. Billy's violent side took control, and he was out for blood.

Lincoln County Sheriff Brady sided with the Murphy-Dolan faction. Brady, born in Ireland but emigrating to the United States as a young man, spent years in the military. After mustering out, he and his wife bought a ranch four miles east of Lincoln. Animosity between Brady and Billy intensified with each passing day.

The day after Tunstall's murder, Billy, along with Dick Brewer, Tunstall's foreman, swore affidavits before Justice of the Peace

87

Ireland-born William James Brady was sheriff of Lincoln County during the Lincoln County War. He ranched four miles east of Lincoln. Brady was blamed for instigating the murder of John Tunstall.
AUTHOR'S COLLECTION

John B. Wilson, naming Dolan, Evans, and sixteen others responsible for the murder. Also that same day, Constable Atanacio Martinez deputized Billy and his friend Fred Waite to help serve warrants. They headed off to Dolan's store.

What they found didn't surprise Billy. A heavily armed group of Dolan men, including Sheriff Brady, waited inside. Brady not only refused to allow the arrests but also placed Martinez, Fred, and Billy under arrest.

Brady threw down on Billy, according to George Coe. Brady demanded, "You little sonofabitch, give me your gun," and Billy hollered back, "Take it, you old sonofabitch!"[1]

Brady grabbed the Winchester '73, Billy's gift from Tunstall. Then Brady marched the three down the street in full sight of the entire town. By doing so, everyone was well aware that Brady defied another Code of the West—don't mess with a man's horse, hat, or gun.

Soon, Martinez was released, but Billy and Fred remained locked up, causing Billy to miss Tunstall's February 22 funeral.

This insult, this final straw, undoubtedly pushed Billy even closer to the edge. Sheriff Brady probably didn't realize it then, but Billy Bonney had put a target on Brady's back.

On March 1, 1878, Justice Wilson appointed Dick Brewer special constable and Billy his deputy. Brewer immediately deputized a posse of fifteen men and called themselves the "Regulators." Their task was to go after Tunstall's murderers and bring them in for justice. Billy was raring to go.

Wasting no time, early the next day, the Regulators left Lincoln and rode east across swelling forested hills toward the Pecos River on a vendetta ride. A few days later, they spotted five men below the crossing of the Rio Peñasco. The five men, part of Dolan's group, split in two and galloped away. The Regulators pursued the party of three—Dick Lloyd, Frank Baker, and Buck Morton (who had shot Tunstall). An estimated 100 shots were fired. After a chase of several miles, Lloyd's horse gave out, and he surrendered. The posse ignored him and rode after Baker and Morton, who, when their horses gave out, dismounted and took cover on the riverbank. When Captain Brewer threatened to burn them out, they surrendered.

As they emerged, hands up, Billy had to be restrained from killing them. He wanted revenge, and he wanted it bad.

Violence between the two factions exploded on April 1, 1878, when Sheriff William Brady rode into town from his outlying ranch. He gathered his deputy George Hindman and three others. The five, with more than a dozen guns between them, made a show of marching shoulder to shoulder down the middle of the street, heading for the courthouse, where Brady was supposedly going to tack up a notice. Why it took five well-armed men to do so was beyond common sense. Were they going to get coffee afterward? Maybe. Nevertheless, the five lawmen made quite a spectacle.

At that same time, Billy and a few of the Regulators were also in town, planning to provide protection for McSween, who was due into Lincoln later that day. From a vantage point and somewhat hidden, Billy and his men watched Brady parading down Main. Billy crouched behind a tall gate at McSween's house.

Concealed, Billy put a borrowed rifle against his shoulder (his prized Winchester '73 was now carried by Brady) and waited. When the five men passed within firing distance, someone shot. Billy swore it wasn't him who fired first. At least a dozen balls struck Brady, who fell dead. George Hindman was shot twice and died in the street. The other three deputies scattered.

For a moment, the town turned deathly quiet. Then Billy sprinted into the street, bent over Brady, and retrieved his rifle. He may have also taken the warrants for his arrest. However, one of the lawmen stepped into the open and fired at Billy, the bullet clipping his hip. Billy hobbled back to the gate's safety.

Presbyterian missionary Reverend Taylor F. Ealy, who had taken cover in his nearby house, reported, "Bullets were flying through town, through and around our house; and we labored and prayed for quieter days, but they did not come."[2]

Although several men on both sides fired their weapons with bullets pinging off posts and walls and into the air, Billy Bonney would be the only one arrested later for Brady's murder.

BLAZER'S MILL

Three days later, on the heels of Brady's death, Billy and Regulators Charlie Bowdre, Frank and George Coe, John Middleton, and Dick Brewer rode south to a Mescalero Apache Indian office known as Blazer's Mill, which also served as a post office, bed-and-breakfast of sorts, as well as a sawmill. A dozen or so Regulators enjoyed staying overnight at Blazer's Mill and had a good meal the next day.

Timing, as they say, is everything. Before the Regulators left the mill, a Dolan supporter for whom they had a warrant rode up to the Indian office. Andrew L. "Buckshot" Roberts had a hard reputation for being mean and for killing at random. Billy saw no problem shooting him right then, but Regulator captain Dick Brewer told him to back off and calm down.

Roberts had worked for Jimmy Dolan but had not been in the posse that killed John Tunstall. Tiring of the tensions and violence that consumed life in Lincoln County, Roberts had decided to pull up stakes and relocate to Las Cruces. He had sold his small ranch and was coming to the post office, hoping that the buyer's check had arrived. Instead, the Regulators had arrived.

Frank Coe spent half an hour talking to Roberts, trying to get him to surrender. When he didn't, Charlie Bowdre told Roberts to throw up his hands. Roberts replied, "Not much, Mary Ann," which was a popular phrase during the Civil War meaning the requesting person was a sissy, also insinuating they were a homosexual—real fighting words then.

With that, the Regulators opened fire. Although hit fatally through the stomach, Roberts backed into Blazer's adobe house, where he discovered a loaded single-shot Springfield rifle, grabbed a mattress, and threw it up as a barrier near the front door. Brewer meanwhile had circled around and crouched behind logs by the entrance. Seeing what he thought was Roberts in the doorway, he snapped off a shot and missed. An expert with a Winchester, Roberts waited until Brewer stuck his head above the logs. He fired. The bullet hit Brewer just above the eyes. He died instantly.

The gunplay lasted about two minutes, resulting in two deaths and everyone else injured. Without exception, each Regulator was injured by one man—Roberts. George Coe later recalled, "With his [Roberts] refusal to throw up his hands, Bowdre's bullet entered Roberts right through the middle, while Roberts' ball glanced off Bowdre's cartridge belt, and with my usual luck, I arrived in time to stop the bullet with my right hand. It knocked the gun out of my hand, took off my trigger finger, and shattered my hand which still bears record of the fight."[3]

Ironically, Roberts and Brewer were buried in the same coffin in a grave near Blazer's house.

Billy freely admitted he did not do much shooting and instead found refuge elsewhere in the house. After the shooting stopped, he and a couple of pals took off for San Patricio, where they spent days resting and healing. George Coe went to Lincoln and sought medical help from Dr. Ealy, who removed his trigger finger and part of another one.

Once recovered, Billy left San Patricio for John Chisum's ranch to see Chisum's niece, Sallie Chisum. Billy would visit whenever he got the chance.

She wrote in her diary that Billy had given her an Indian tobacco sack and some candy hearts. A prolific writer, Billy penned her several letters, the most noted one while he was pinned down at McSween's house in Lincoln. There's no evidence she ever received the missive.

Shortly after they left Blazer's Mill, a gang of Dolan's men searching for Billy and the Regulators rampaged through San

George Coe shows off his wounds from Blazer's Mill. He lost his trigger finger when a bullet bounced off Bowdre's buckle.

Sallie Chisum enjoyed Billy's visits to her uncle's ranch near Roswell. Billy would bring her candy and perform riding tricks for her.

Patricio, tearing down fences, riding horses through stores, and killing one man.

Billy's anger continued to boil.

THE BIG KILLING—THE FEUD NEARS AN END

"Reports from Lincoln County indicate a renewal of hostilities between adverse factions," reported the *Las Vegas Gazette* on June 22, 1878. "Both parties are in the field and a collision is imminent. If they should succeed in completely destroying each other the result would be hailed by all good citizens."

Lincoln County War

The Lincoln County War, also known as the Big Killing or the Five Days War, was a complex, Gordian knot of intrigue, intense loyalty, treachery, killings, betrayal, deviousness, and outright greed and corruption. Partly, it boiled down to a matter of the Irish influence in Lincoln versus the Englishman John Tunstall and his friends. That particular conflict was brought over with them when they immigrated. Many tomes have been written about this major event in Southwest history. Not willing to rehash the details here but instead keeping the focus on Billy, much of the minutiae has been condensed for this telling. Plenty of other writings offer further information.

The violence all came to a head on July 15, 1878. Dolan and his men, now including Jesse Evans and his gang, and John Kinney (leader of the Boys) and his gang, as well as New Mexico Territorial Governor Samuel Axtell, a sheriff, a district attorney, a judge, the Fort Stanton colonel, a gang of killers from Texas, and the Santa Fe Ring, drew together. Behind Billy stood the Regulators and the law of the gun.

Billy and his close friend Tom O. Folliard, along with at least a dozen Regulators, Alexander McSween, his wife Susan, her sister, and five children, took refuge in McSween's rambling, U-shaped adobe in Lincoln.

The two sides exchanged gunfire for three days, pinning down the occupants of the McSween home. No one dared go outside to use the privy or get freshwater. Squeezed into the house, they coped with chamber pots full to overflowing, dwindling food supplies, and cranky children who created crankier women. The odors of sweaty men in July heat, the full chamber pots, and cooking food filled every nook and cranny. Tensions sizzled.

Tom O. Folliard, three years older than Billy, was best friends with the legendary outlaw. His photo is a victim of silver corrosion; thus, his lower jaw looks diseased. It was not. Tom is buried next to Billy.
AUTHOR'S COLLECTION

Fort Stanton

Established in 1855, Fort Stanton may be one of the most intact nineteenth-century military forts in the country. This 240-acre site is best known for its roles in the Indian Wars and the Civil War.

Over its 160-year history, Fort Stanton has witnessed westward expansion, the lawless days of Billy the Kid and the Lincoln County War, the tuberculosis epidemic that peaked in the 1920s, the New Deal–era Civilian Conservation Corps, and the internment of German sailors during World War II. Fort Stanton's twelve-building parade ground and buildings appear much as they did in the mid-1800s. Currently, the fort is open to the public.

Seeing no way to end this, Susan McSween sent for the army out of nearby Fort Stanton. Surely, they would help. Commander Colonel Nathan Dudley replied this feud was a civilian matter, not an army one. Then another woman from town walked nine miles to the fort and begged the soldiers to stop the fighting. She could not leave her house for wood or water; her children cowered in their house, afraid to go outside. Her tears softened Dudley's heart.

Giving in, Dudley sent a private to see what was happening. The soldier narrowly missed being struck by a bullet and, rattled, scampered back to the fort, telling the colonel he had been fired on. Between Susan McSween's pleas, the plight of the poor woman with children, and thinking the town was attacking the army, Dudley sent troops armed with a cannon and Gatling gun to quell the fighting.

By day five of the standoff, Dudley threatened to turn the artillery on McSween's house if Billy and his group didn't surrender. Not waiting any longer, a couple of Dolan's men splashed a bucket of coal oil against a house wall and put a match to it.

Fortunately, adobe doesn't burn well, and only the wooden parts of the house went up at first. Susan, her sister, and all five children were allowed to leave unharmed.

The fire spread slowly but steadily. Beginning in the northwest corner, flames took seven hours to totally engulf the building.

Billy, taking charge, shouted words of encouragement and offered escape alternatives, although there weren't many. They could stay and burn, surrender and be shot right there, or make a run for it. Billy and his men decided to wait until dark to try an escape, knowing a few wouldn't make it—better than none surviving, which was a sure thing if they remained in the house.

Just as smoke billowed into the last unscathed room, the sun set, and Billy gathered the five remaining men. Steeling themselves for the inevitable but hoping for the best, the Regulators scrambled out of a back window. The first man out was shot and killed, but that brave act provided enough distraction for two more men, then Billy and Folliard, the last out of the inferno, to bolt behind the house. The four survivors plunged into the Rio Bonito yards away and took cover in the bushes.

Alexander McSween had spent considerable time in his house muttering to himself over the past five days, totally indecisive and at times irrational. The urge to stop running away from his opponents and his conviction that he might not win the battle clouded his decision making. He decided to surrender. Arms up, white flag in hand, he stepped outside. Bullets plowed into him before he got five feet from the door. Perhaps his ill-timed surrender was a sacrifice that brought opportunity for the other men to escape.

Amazingly, most men in the house lived, including Billy, who managed to outlast the five-day standoff.

"When the Kid jumped out of the burning house," said historian Bob Boze Bell, "he became the most famous person in New Mexico."[4]

Reveling in their victory, Dolan's men broke into Tunstall's store, literally next to the burning house, and helped themselves to all the whiskey and goods they could steal. All this was under the cheerful and patriotic eyes of the U.S. Army.

A coroner's jury, composed of all Dolan men, pronounced that McSween and the other dead Regulators' cause of death was "resisting arrest." Case closed.

With Tunstall and McSween dead and John Chisum turning his allegiance toward Dolan, the feud was over. Peace returned to Lincoln.

BACK TO RUSTLING

But there was no peace for Billy, who was still determined to revenge Tunstall's death. Frustrated by the lack of "fair" law but needing an income, Billy returned to doing what he did best—rustling cattle. George Coe told Billy that he and George's cousin Frank were tired of the outlaw life and always running. They were moving up to Colorado to start fresh. Billy replied, "Well, boys, you may all do exactly as you please. As for me, I propose to stay right here in this country, steal [*sic*] myself to living, and plant every one of the mob who murdered Tunstall if they don't get the drop on me first."[5]

But still, the Coes' departure hurt. Even his friends Charlie Bowdre and Doc Scurlock left to go work on the Maxwell Ranch, putting the Lincoln County feud behind them. Billy turned to Tom Folliard and Fred Waite for companionship.

Oddly, during the standoff in July at McSween's house, a quick cease-fire was ordered so that mail could be delivered to the house. There, McSween bought stamps, and Billy mailed a letter to Sallie.

Later, Sallie wrote to Billy, telling him her uncle James Chisum was herding a large group of cattle from the Chisum ranch north to free grazing ranges near Tascosa in the Texas Panhandle. Billy decided to follow and meet up with Sallie en route.

Sallie wrote in her diary, "Regulators come up with us at Red River Springs on the 25 Sept 1878."[6] Billy and his group were driving a large remuda of horses they had gathered to sell to Texas clients.

Following this rendezvous in the Texas Panhandle, Billy and Sallie parted ways and never saw each other again.

At Tascosa, Dr. Henry Hoyt, a twenty-four-year-old doctor from the East visiting the Southwest, enjoyed Billy's company, attending dances together and playing cards. "Billy was an expert at most Western sports, except drinking."[7] Neither Hoyt nor Billy were drinkers, both sharing an aversion to alcohol. "Billy and the boys were just part of the town," he said in an interview. "Selling and trading, drinking, gambling, racing horses and shooting at targets."[8]

Hoyt recalled a time when he and Billy were attending a dance at Casimero Romero's dance hall in Tascosa. In order to attend, everyone had to agree to "park their weapons at the door." As the evening wore on, the two stepped out of the thick-walled adobe building and walked across the road.

On the way back, Hoyt challenged Billy to a footrace. Both men took off at a dead run. Nearing the doorway, which had a typical threshold about a foot above ground level, Hoyt stopped. Billy did not. He rushed headlong through the doorway, failed to step over the threshold, tripped, and sprawled belly first onto the dance floor.

"Quicker than scat," said Hoyt, "those four men were back-to-back around Billy, with a gun in each hand. They thought the way he came in that trouble was on."[9]

Billy sheepishly stood, then dusted off his clothes. Fred Waite, Henry Brown, John Middleton, and Tom Folliard were asked to leave and had to promise to never ever again bring in weapons that they supposedly had already "parked."

Not one to miss irony, when Hoyt was ready to continue his adventures in the fall of 1878 and leave Tascosa, Billy gave him an Arabian sorrel named Dandy Dick with "BB" branded on the left hip. Billy even scratched out a bill of sale for Hoyt. Much later,

Hoyt learned that the BB stood for "William Brady" and that he had been "gifted" the same horse on which the unlucky sheriff had ridden into Lincoln on April 1, 1878.

MEETING PAT GARRETT

"Billy came to Tascosa in the Panhandle. He stayed at my camp a month," stated a man who worked on a ranch in West Texas. "He stayed all around there among the cow men until spring and then went back to New Mexico. Then he went to stealing cattle . . . would come over south of Tascosa and get them and drive them away. The cow men got tired of it and got Pat Garrett to come over there and talk to him."[10]

A man of questionable morals and values, Patrick Floyd Garrett was once a good friend of Billy, even rustling cattle in Texas together. Paulita Maxwell said at one time there was no one closer than those two.
AUTHOR'S COLLECTION

It is generally thought that Billy first met Pat Garrett at the Chisum Ranch in 1878. Eyewitnesses claim Billy and Pat Garrett became "thick as thieves" and knew each other quite well. They were a mismatched pair; six-foot-four Pat Garrett was known as Juan Largo or "Tall John," while five-foot-seven Billy answered to "Little Casino" due to his card-playing abilities. Their friendship turned heads as they attended *bailes* and gambled together. How well they knew each other is up for debate, but both men hung around Fort Sumner and appeared to be inseparable, best friends. They even rustled Texas cattle in Tascosa and nearby Mobeetie together.

The fall of 1878 held many changes in the political structure of the New Mexico Territory. Most important to Billy was the removal of Governor Samuel Axtell by President Rutherford B. Hayes. Former Civil War general Lew Wallace took over in October.

Lewis Wallace, born in 1827, was a lawyer, a Union general in the Civil War, a governor, a politician, a diplomat, and an author. After serving in the U.S. Army for many years, Wallace resigned in 1865 and briefly served as a major general in the Mexican army. Returning to the United States, Wallace was appointed governor of the New Mexico Territory. On November 13, 1878, Wallace declared amnesty for all parties involved in the Lincoln County War—all except those with an indictment against them, which Billy Bonney had. But Billy didn't realize he had been singled out. Not yet anyway.

CHAPTER TEN

BETRAYED BY GARRETT AND WALLACE

"The motive behind Pat Garrett's relentless pursuit of the Kid was that his death meant money and the office of sheriff of Lincoln County."

—MIGUEL ANTONIO OTERO,
AUTHOR OF *THE REAL BILLY THE KID*
WITH NEW LIGHT ON THE LINCOLN COUNTY WAR

AN EYEWITNESS

BY LATE 1878, BILLY AND SEVERAL OF THE MCSWEEN MEN HAD returned to Lincoln, where they proceeded to take control of the town. In February 1879, Billy and his former nemesis Jesse Evans agreed to call a truce. Instead of fighting each other, they would join forces. To celebrate, both sides went drinking in every saloon in town. Billy, not an imbiber, stayed sober.

Susan McSween had hired a Santa Fe lawyer, one-armed and highly strung Huston Chapman, to file charges against Colonel Dudley at Fort Stanton. She accused the officer of the murder of her husband, Alexander. On February 18, 1879, the day Chapman arrived in Lincoln to meet Mrs. McSween, he encountered Evans's and Billy's inebriated mob on the street. They suggested he dance; he refused and was shot twice in the chest by Billy Campbell and James Dolan. The shots were at such close range that Chapman's shirt and jacket caught fire. He died after uttering, "My God. I am killed!"

Billy was an eyewitness. Knowing he would be implicated if not accused of the murder, Billy and Tom Folliard hightailed it immediately out of town, heading for San Patricio.

Governor Wallace, weary of the killings in Lincoln, formed a posse, hunting for anyone involved in Chapman's murder. Billy got wind of it. He was an eyewitness, and if he played his cards right (told everything he knew), the governor would most likely grant him a pardon from all offenses, including his involvement in the Lincoln County War.

To Billy, Wallace wrote, "Testify before the grand jury and the trial court and convict the murderer of Chapman, and I will let you go scot-free with a pardon in your pocket for all your misdeeds."[1]

In March, Billy wrote the governor asking for a meeting. Two days later, he received a letter from Wallace suggesting a meeting at Squire Wilson's house in Lincoln. Wallace wrote, [On March 17] "I heard a knock at the door, and I called out 'Come in.' The door opened somewhat slowly and carefully, and there stood the young fellow generally known as the Kid, Winchester in his right hand, revolver in his left."[2]

Wallace and Billy concocted a plan where Billy and Folliard would be "arrested" in order to put them under protective custody before the trial. A few days later, Lincoln County Sheriff George Kimbrell and his posse rode into San Patricio and placed Billy and Folliard under house arrest at the Lincoln home of Juan Patrón.

House arrest wasn't so bad. Most of the time, Billy played cards, wrote letters, and sang along with the women and a few men of Lincoln who serenaded under his window. Wallace, who stayed next door, was mystified by Billy's popularity.

Lewis Wallace was a Civil War general who had a passion for writing. While New Mexico territorial governor, he penned the novel *Ben Hur.*

"I heard singing and music the other night," he wrote to the secretary of the interior, Carl Schurz. "Going to the door I found the minstrels of the village actually serenading the fellow in his prison."[3]

According to Ash Upson and Pat Garrett, "[The Kid and Folliard] led a gay life at the house of Patrón. Plenty to eat and drink, the best of cigars, and a game of poker with anyone, friend or stranger, who chanced to visit them. The Kid was cheerful and seemingly contented. His hand was small and his wrist large. When a friend entered, he would advance, slip his hand from the irons, stretch it out to shake hands and remark: 'I don't wish to disgrace you, sir,' or 'you don't get a chance to steal my jewelry, old fellow.'"[4]

After spending over two months "in jail," Billy testified in May in a military court of inquiry examining the actions of Fort Stanton's Colonel Nathan Dudley during the Lincoln County War. Despite Billy's eyewitness testimony, Dudley was exonerated, and the two people tried in civilian courts were acquitted.

Governor Wallace's request to pardon Billy fell on hostile, deaf ears. District Attorney William Rynerson, a ruthless prosecutor, wanted Billy punished to the full extent of the law. A solid member of the Santa Fe Ring and Dolan's close friend, Rynerson had no intention of honoring the governor's request.

With the acquittals, Billy saw the proverbial handwriting on the wall. No way he'd receive that promised pardon. In fact, he reasoned, he would be arrested next, put on trial, and found guilty.

Determined to escape the hangman's noose, Billy Bonney and Tom Folliard hightailed it out of Lincoln on June 17, 1879, under the darkness of a waning crescent moon.

BACK AT FORT SUMNER

For the next several months, Billy surfaced in northern and eastern New Mexico, randomly visiting friends all over the territory. There seemed to be no particular order or purpose to his rides. He would simply show up, stay for a bit, and then leave. More often, he visited the mining town of White Oaks and then Fort Sumner. The old fort had become a conglomeration of Mexican and Hispanic ranchers and farmers as well as cowboys and men lying low from the law. Located strategically between cattle ranches in the Texas Panhandle and the military beef markets of both Fort Stanton and the Mescalero Reservation, Fort Sumner proved to be a retreat and rest stop for Billy.

Fort Sumner, eighty miles northeast of Lincoln and abandoned by the army in 1868, included officers' houses, outbuildings, and hundreds of acres of land owned by Pete Maxwell. Nestled on the edge of the Staked Plains, also known as Llano Estacado, in eastern New Mexico, the compound boasted a lively and vibrant society, a perfect incubator for crime. For Billy, this old fort turned outlaw oasis was full of rocking hilarity in the saloons of Beaver Smith and Bob Hargrove. Cowboys, sheepmen, and outlaws congregated there. The best part was that the "law" was 100 miles away, where the county sheriff and his deputy had more than they could handle in raucous Las Vegas, New Mexico, a booming railroad town far from Fort Sumner. They rarely visited.

Enjoying a wide circle of friends, Billy more and more often stayed in Fort Sumner, particularly at Yginio Garcia's house. His true friends were Hispanic sheepherders whose animals grazed on the wide expanses of grassy fields. Billy was always welcomed at their camps. Not quite as true were the Anglo cattlemen, who regarded Billy with a bit of reserve. Would he rustle their cattle and sell them in White Oaks? They were never quite sure. Although most of the Regulators had located away from the area, Charlie Bowdre remained, as did Tom Folliard. For the next couple of years, Charlie and Tom stayed at his side and are buried side by side with Billy.

At Fort Sumner and as safe from the law as could be, Billy enjoyed sleeping well at night, with or without a señorita at his side. Beaver Smith's Saloon was the rowdiest of the two drinking establishments, and this was where Billy often dealt monte or played other card games. His favorite pastimes were dancing and singing. And there was a lot of that.

Here is where Billy's smile, good humor, lively dancing, and gentlemanly manners fluttered most female hearts. He loved dancing, and the dancers loved him. "Billy the Kid, I may tell you," Paulita Maxwell, rumored to be Billy's last girlfriend, told writer Walter Noble Burns in 1924, "fascinated many women. In every *placeta* [little plaza] in the Pecos, some little *señorita* was proud to be known as his *querida* [sweetheart]. At least three girls in Fort Sumner were mad about him. One is now a respected

Following Billy the Kid map. As Billy rode throughout the territory, he attracted women and had a *novia* in almost every village.

MAP COURTESY OF GUS WALKER ESTATE AND PATTI HERSEY

matron of Las Vegas, New Mexico. Another, who died long ago, had a daughter who lived to be eight years old and whose striking resemblance to the famous outlaw filled her mother's heart with pride."

Paulita reminisced, "Fort Sumner was a gay little place. The weekly dance was an event and pretty girls from Santa Rosa, Puerto de Luna, Anton Chico and from towns and ranches fifty miles away drove in to attend it. Billy the Kid cut quite a gallant figure at these affairs. He was not handsome, but he had a certain sort of boyish good looks. He was always smiling and good-natured and very polite and danced remarkably well, and the little Mexican beauties made eyes at him behind their fans and used all their coquetries to capture him and were very vain of his attentions."[5]

CHAPTER ELEVEN

BECOMING BILLY THE KID

"He may have discovered that out here, where no one knows you, you are free to invent a new life."
— FINTAN O'TOOLE, *THE NEW YORKER*
(DECEMBER 28, 1998–JANUARY 4, 1999), 97.

KILLING JOE GRANT

IT WAS ALSO HERE IN FORT SUMNER THAT BILLY KILLED HIS second man. In January 1880, Billy and his friends, along with Jim Chisum and some of his cowboys, entered Bob Hargrove's saloon. Joe Grant, also called Texas Red, was drunk and challenged Billy to a deadly shooting contest. He kept pestering Billy and boasted, "I bet twenty-five dollars I kill a man today before you do."

He wobbled over to a Chisum cowhand, grabbed his pistol out of its holster, and began smashing bottles across the saloon. He then turned the gun on Jim Chisum, threatening to shoot him.

Was this cowboy another bully like Windy Cahill? Billy vowed not to be blindsided, taken down again. An expert with weapons, Billy asked to see the pistol. Spinning the cylinder, he noticed three shells had been fired and rolled the cylinder until the next two shots would misfire on empty chambers. When Grant moved toward Chisum, Billy told him, "You got the wrong sow by the ear."

"That's a lie," Texas Red hollered, twisting to aim at Billy, who turned away. With his back to Grant and hearing the click of a spent shell, Billy spun around and fired three shots into the bully's chin. Grant died immediately.

With no real law at the fort and since what everyone witnessed was clearly self-defense, Billy was never charged with Grant's murder. However, things were about to change.

Hearing reports that the law was on his tail, Billy wrote to Wallace again, proclaiming his innocence in shooting Sheriff Brady.

In reply, the governor announced a $500 reward for Billy's capture.

Billy Bonney versus Billy the Kid

Billy Bonney answered to various names during his twenty years. The one that stuck was Billy the Kid. But where did this come from? Many men who were young looking, especially those who rode alongside older men, were called "Kid." It wasn't until December 3, 1880, that W. S. Koogler, co-owner of the *Las Vegas Gazette*, wrote a letter of complaint to Governor Lew Wallace about "the powerful gang of outlaws harassing the stockmen of the Pecos and Panhandle country, and terrorizing the people of Fort Sumner and vicinity."

"This army of outlaws," he went on to write, "is under the leadership of 'Billy the Kid,' a desperate cuss, who is eligible for the post of captain of any crowd, no matter how mean and lawless."[1]

From that point forward, other newspapers used the moniker Billy the Kid. Thus the legend began.

Tired of the rustling raids led by Billy and the other cattle thieves, large ranchers like John Chisum and Captain Joseph C. Lea urged Pat Garrett to move to Lincoln and to run for county sheriff. Much to Billy's chagrin, Garrett won the election in early November. A few weeks later, Garrett set out to round up Billy and his outlaw sidekicks. For the next eight months, Garrett tailed the Kid like a persistent bulldog.[2]

"Before that fateful night [July 14, 1881]," said historian Marc Simmons, "there was not much in Garrett's career to suggest he was 'headed for a place in the history books.' Alabama-born in 1850, he worked as a cowboy and buffalo hunter in Texas. By 1878, he had drifted to the Pecos in eastern New Mexico. He ran for sheriff of wild Lincoln County in the fall of 1880. His election put him on a collision course with Billy."[3]

STINKING SPRINGS MELEE

Deputy-elect Garrett was determined to find Billy and either shoot him or bring him in. The $500 bounty on Billy's head was a great incentive. Garrett rested up in Puerto de Luna, spending the day with his men eating and sharing stories. On December 17, 1880, Garrett decided to leave the warmth of Grzelachowski's store in Puerto de Luna with his posse in the early afternoon before a storm hit. They arrived at Pablo Beaubien's ranch, where Garrett learned Billy was hiding out at Fort Sumner. The posse moved on, looking forward to capturing Billy but also looking over their shoulders at the incoming storm. Twenty-five miles above Fort Sumner, the blizzard hit. They stopped for food and to warm their hands but pushed on around midnight.

Laser focused on his quarry, Garrett and his posse trudged through waist-deep snow heading south to Fort Sumner against one of the worst blizzards in decades. Intensely cold, some of the men walked in order to save their horses. Along the way, at least two men developed frostbite, and all of them suffered from below-zero temperatures. But they were determined to make it to Fort Sumner by sunrise.

Reaching Fort Sumner in time, they took positions in the shadows around the fort's former hospital, where Manuela

Bowdre lived. They figured that's where Billy would go. Garrett forced a Hispanic boy to take a note to Billy's gang that said Garrett and his men had left and Billy was safe to return. The message was delivered.

On the night of December 19, thinking something wasn't right, Billy and his men sauntered toward town. Feeling wary, Billy dropped to the back of the group to pull a chaw of tobacco and have another scan of the area. Using tobacco probably saved his life that night.

As the group rode close to the hospital building, Garrett yelled, "Halt!" Folliard reached for his pistol, but Garrett fired a deadly shot into Folliard's chest. Billy and his men raced into the dark snow and out of town. Forty-five minutes later, Billy's best friend, Tom Folliard died. He was twenty-two.

Folliard's death was a grim warning to the outlaws they would receive no reprieve from Sheriff Pat Garrett.

Fighting through one of the century's worst blizzards, Billy the Kid, Charlie Bowdre, Dave Rudabaugh, Billy Wilson, and Tom Pickett raced out of town east, plowing through knee-deep snow to an old sheepherder's rock-lined shack, known as Stinking Springs.

Once there, the men stayed inside, knowing a posse was right behind. Freezing cold with mounting snow, for extra warmth and a quick escape, they brought two horses inside, one of which was Billy's, known to be sturdy and fast.

Garrett and his posse followed through drifting snow and stopped in a ditch that was mere yards from the shack. He had questioned people in Fort Sumner as to Billy's clothing and knew he wore his favored sugarloaf sombrero with a green hatband.

"Just at daybreak Charlie Bowdre came to the door and stepped out," the *Las Vegas Gazette* reported on December 27, 1880. He wore a hat like Billy the Kid's and was mistaken for him. Someone fired, and Bowdre staggered and then, bracing himself up for a moment against the door post, stepped into the house. He told his companions that he was badly wounded and could not assist them any and wanted to go out, calling to the men outside. Bowdre stepped out again and started forward to give himself up when he reeled a little and said, "I wish ——," and while making an effort to express his desire, he fell dead close by where one of the besiegers was lying concealed."[4]

Hours later, the men inside were cold, hungry, and desperate to escape. They slowly pulled the outside horses' reins toward the house. Garrett, knowing the men would try an escape by jumping on their mounts and galloping off, shot the horse closest to the door, effectively blocking any escape they had.

With Bowdre dead, no way to get to the horses, and everyone suffering through hours of freezing cold and hunger, Billy and his friends surrendered. Since Fort Sumner could not house the dangerous captives, Garrett rounded up the prisoners and headed toward Las Vegas, New Mexico. From there, they would go to Santa Fe, where they would await trial. Later, with a change of venue, Billy would be sent to La Mesilla, where Dolan and his cronies ruled the court.

On their way to Las Vegas, on Christmas Eve, Billy arrived at Fort Sumner, where Manuela Bowdre was distraught with grief. She even clobbered one of the posse members with a branding iron. Hoping to appease her, Garrett offered to buy Charlie a new set of clothes in which to be buried and also to pay for his coffin. She was not assuaged and continued to mourn loudly.

After lunch at Beaver Smith's Saloon, Deluvina Maxwell, Pete Maxwell's older Navajo servant who was quite fond of the Kid, asked that Billy be granted one last good-bye to his *novia* Paulita Maxwell. Garrett agreed.

Although handcuffed to Dave Rudabaugh, Billy was able to say a proper farewell. One of the posse later said, "The lovers embraced, and she gave Billy one of those soul kisses the novelists tell you about, till it being time to hit the road for Vegas, we had to pull them apart, much against our wishes, for you know, all the world loves a lover."[5]

Along the way, Garrett, the posse, Billy, Rudabaugh, Wilson, and Pickett stopped on December 25, 1880, at Alexander Grzelchowski's mercantile in Puerto de Luna, where they feasted on a hearty Yule dinner. Billy and the Polish immigrant had enjoyed each other's company many times before. In fact, Billy had attended dances there when he wasn't trading (and stealing) horses.

Leaving Puerto de Luna, the party arrived in Las Vegas in the late afternoon of December 26, 1880, without much fanfare. By the next morning, however, large crowds gathered at the jail. Half simply wanted to see the famous outlaw; the other half wanted to get Rudabaugh out in order to hang him.

Dave Rudabaugh, born in 1854, began his outlaw career in Arkansas in the early 1870s. He was part of a band of outlaws who robbed and participated in cattle rustling along with Milton Yarberry (who later went on to become Albuquerque's first town marshal and got himself hanged) and "Mysterious" Dave Mather. Rudabaugh received the moniker "Dirty" Dave due to his penchant for not washing his clothes or his person.

After killing a rancher, he fled to South Dakota and became a stagecoach robber. In Las Vegas, New Mexico, he threw in with the Dodge City Gang, which controlled the town.

The angry citizens of Las Vegas ran the Gang and Rudabaugh out of town. That's when Rudabaugh rode to Fort Sumner and met Billy. But before leaving Las Vegas, Rudabaugh had killed a popular jailer while trying to free J. J. Webb from prison. Now that he was back again, citizens were ready to take justice into their own hands. Lucky for him, Rudabaugh remained safe in jail.

A *Las Vegas Gazette* reporter was allowed to interview Billy as he changed into new clothes before taking the train to Santa Fe.

Bonney was light and chipper and very communicative, laughing, joking, and chatting with bystanders.

"You appear to take it easy," the reporter said.

"Yes! What's the use of looking on the gloomy side of everything? The laugh's on me this time," he said.

He was the attraction of the show, and as he stood there, lightly kicking the toes of his boots on the stone pavement to keep his feet warm, one would scarcely mistrust that he was the hero of the Forty Thieves *romance which this paper has been running in serial form for six weeks or more.*

"Well," he said of the crowd of bystanders staring at him, "perhaps some of them will think of me half man now; everyone seems to think I was some kind of animal."[6]

The same reporter wrote, "There was nothing very mannish about him in appearance, for he looked and acted a mere boy . . . looking like a schoolboy, with the traditional silky fuzz on his upper lip, clear blue eyes with a roguish snap about them; light hair and complexion. . . . He has agreeable and winning ways."[7] Billy had turned nineteen in May.

From the train about to leave for Santa Fe, Billy spoke with another reporter, saying, "I made my living by gambling but that was the only way I could live. They wouldn't let me settle down: if they had I wouldn't be here today." He continued, "Chisum got me into all this trouble and then wouldn't help me out. If it hadn't been for the dead horse in the doorway [at Stinking Springs] I wouldn't be here. I would have ridden my bay mare and taken my chances of escaping."

The reporter added, "As the train rolled out, he lifted his hat and invited us to call and see him in Santa Fe, calling out 'Adios.'"[8] This was Billy's first train ride.

On the train, he enjoyed a delay at Glorieta Pass due to snow. To help pass time, Billy ordered a piece of apple pie, and to the amusement of the children nearby, he placed the entire slice into his mouth. He closed his mouth and then opened it. The pie was still there in one piece! The children squealed with delight while mothers tsked. Garrett and the posse laughed alongside Billy.

Sheriff-elect Garrett deposited his prisoners with the marshal in Santa Fe. There, they experienced the first of many injustices right off. Garrett ordered food for Billy and Rudabaugh, but the jailer ate it all.

Chapter Twelve

"A Man More Sinned against Than Sinning"

"He was compelled to live the life of an outlaw, though his outlawry consisted more of stealing cattle than killing."
—George Coe, Billy's friend

On New Year's Day, the Kid wrote yet another letter to Governor Wallace from his jail cell in Santa Fe. "I would like to see you a few moments if You can Spare time." He then wrote three more letters.[1]

All went unanswered.

The Kid passed three months in the Santa Fe jail mainly by writing to Governor Lew Wallace. For most of that time, Wallace was traveling in the East, unaware of the Kid's letters. And Billy was unaware Wallace was busy promoting his book *Ben Hur*. The Kid's third letter to the governor was filled with mistrust. He talked about how Judge Ira Leonard did not hold up his end of a bargain, too. "He promised to come and see me on his way back, but he did not fulfill his promise. It looks to me like I am getting left in the cold."[2]

When not writing letters, the Kid helped his cell mates Dave Rudabaugh, Billy Wilson, and Choctaw Kelly attempt to dig their way out of the adobe jail. Depositing the dirt and rocks into their mattresses kept their secret until they were nearly through the wall. An inside informant told the deputy U.S. marshal, who immediately separated the prisoners. The Kid was put into solitary confinement and shackled to the floor of a cell "where even the light of day is denied admittance and only when some of the jailers or officers enter can he be seen at all."[3]

However, a few visitors were allowed to see the Kid. Miguel Otero, whose father was a prominent politician and businessman, said, "In Santa Fe we [he and brother Page] were allowed to see the Kid in jail, taking him cigarette papers, tobacco, chewing gum, candy, pies, and nuts. He was very fond of sweets and asked us to bring all we could."[4] Otero would later become the first Hispanic governor (1897–1906) of the New Mexico Territory.

Billy's last letter to Wallace, sent on March 27, again fell on deaf ears, though his growing urgency was palpable. "For the last time I ask. Will you keep your promise? I start below [to La Mesilla] tomorrow. Send answer by bearer. —Yours Resp., W. Bonney."[5]

The Kid never got the answer he was waiting for. On Sunday, March 28, 1881, Billy Wilson and lawyer Ira Leonard accompanied Billy to the train station in Lamy, New Mexico, south of Santa Fe. They were originally scheduled to leave Saturday, but due to scheduling issues, they didn't roll out until Sunday. This change of plans disrupted a party of more than thirty men waiting for them at the southern terminus of Rincon, thirty-six miles north of La Mesilla.

The intentions of the crowd were unclear. Did they intend to lynch the Kid or free him? To keep the prisoners safe, a deputy U.S. marshal and the Santa Fe chief of police hurried the prisoners into a saloon's back room. At long last, the marshal was able to disperse the crowd without bloodshed.

From Rincon, the Kid and his party boarded a stagecoach and proceeded to La Mesilla. The *Daily New Mexican* reported, "At

Las Cruces an inquisitive mob gathered around the coach, and someone asked, 'which is Billy the Kid?' The Kid himself answered by placing his hand on Judge Leonard's shoulder, saying 'This is the man.'"[6]

His bravado faded when he realized quite a number of Lincoln County men were there to testify against him.

STANDING TRIAL IN LA MESILLA

The Kid faced two murder counts, one for the unlawful death of Andrew "Buckshot" Roberts at Blazer's Mill and the other for Lincoln County Sheriff William Brady on Lincoln's street. The trial was held in the same room on the La Mesilla Plaza where the Gadsden Purchase was signed thirty years earlier. On April 3, 1881, he was arraigned for the murder of Buckshot Roberts, and Judge Leonard was assigned as defense. Three days later, that charge was dropped because the shooting did not occur on federal land, and therefore he could not be tried in a federal court.

The Kid must have breathed a short sigh of relief when that charge was removed.

His next trial began on April 8, 1881. Simon Newcomb had replaced William Rynerson as district attorney. Unfortunately for the Kid, court-appointed Ira Leonard recused himself as defense lawyer and was replaced by John Bail and Albert Jennings Fountain (the former newspaper editor, now a lawyer), who was a close friend of Jimmy Dolan. Neither Bail nor Fountain knew much about the Kid.

During the trial, the Kid swore he had not even fired at Brady during the ambush but rather at Deputy Mathews, against whom he had a special grudge. The jury paid no attention—a day later, they found him guilty and sentenced him to hang.[7]

When the jury returned the guilty verdict, the judge asked the Kid if he had anything to say. He did not, stating later that he knew everyone would think he was lying and therefore there was no need to waste words.

On April 13, Judge Bristol, a crony of Dolan, directed the prisoner to be turned over to Lincoln County Sheriff Pat Garrett and to be confined to jail in Lincoln until May 13. On that day, between the hours of nine and three, "The said William Bonney, alias Kid, alias William Antrim [was to] be hanged by the neck until his body be dead."[8]

Obviously shaken and embittered but not surprised, the Kid summed up his situation to a *Mesilla News* reporter: "I think it is a dirty mean advantage to take of me, considering my situation and knowing I could not defend myself by word or act. . . . Think it hard I should be the only one to suffer the extreme penalty of the law."[9]

A week later, a Las Vegas, New Mexico, reporter told the governor, "He appears to look for you to save his neck."

"Yes," Wallace replied, "but I can't see how a fellow like him should expect any clemency from me."[10]

AT LINCOLN WAITING TO HANG

The six-day wagon ride back to Lincoln was uneventful. Before leaving La Mesilla, the Kid spoke with a *Mesilla Times* reporter about his trip to Lincoln. The Kid shrugged. "If mob law is going to rule, better dismiss judge, sheriff, etc., and let all take chances alike. I expect to be lynched in going to Lincoln. Advise persons never to engage in killing."[11]

Assigned to guard and ride alongside the Kid were men he hated the most: Billy Mathews, John Kinney (former leader of the Boys), and Lincoln County Deputy Sheriff Bob Olinger, along with five special deputies. The entire party, armed to the teeth, fingers on their triggers, were the kind of men who never hesitated to kill. And they were itching to kill the Kid, especially Olinger.

The Kid was handcuffed, shackled, and chained to the back-seat of the wagon. Kinney sat beside him, Olinger on the seat facing him—giving him a good position to constantly harass him.

Despite his services as a lawman, Robert Olinger was a "bully with a badge" and touted to be a serial murder. Even his mother didn't like him.
AUTHOR'S COLLECTION

Mathews sat facing Kinney, and the others rode horses alongside and behind. All the way to Lincoln, Olinger taunted the Kid. "Your days are short, Kid. I can see that rope around your neck now."[12] Six days later, they arrived in Lincoln without incident despite the Kid's premonitions.

The Kid's prison cell was Lawrence Murphy's former bedroom on the second floor of the Dolan store. One window overlooked the main street and another out into the yard. In the cell, his chains were fastened to the floor. Once the Kid was settled in, Garrett dismissed all the guards except Deputy Sheriffs Bob Olinger and James W. Bell.

Bell, a former Texas Ranger and current resident of White Oaks, New Mexico (one of Billy's major hangouts), was appointed "special constable" by the Lincoln County Commissioners on April 4. He was paid $65.50 ($1,730 today) and assigned to guard the Kid until his hanging date on May 13.

In terms of personality, Bob Olinger was directly the opposite of Bell. Olinger was described as "two hundred pounds of bone and muscle, six feet tall, round as a huge tree trunk, with a regular gorilla-like chest." He despised the Kid, whom he blamed for killing his friend at the McSween shootout. At every opportunity, Olinger belittled and tormented the Kid, and at one point, Garrett told him to "lay off the Kid." He didn't.

According to an acquaintance, Olinger declared that the Kid "was a cur and that every man he had killed had been murdered in cold blood and without the slightest chance of defending himself."

Pat Garrett said, "There was a reciprocal hatred between those two, and neither attempted to disguise or conceal his antipathy for the other."[13]

Olinger delighted in flaunting a shotgun that, under Billy's nose, he would load, then unload, then load again. He'd then make a show of placing it in a room across the hall, just out of the Kid's reach, a taunt that would prove to be his downfall.

And one day, it happened. Sheriff Pat Garrett rode out of town headed to White Oaks to do two things: collect taxes and buy lumber for the Kid's gallows. He left Olinger and Bell in charge. On April 28, 1881, Olinger walked five prisoners across the street to the Wortley Hotel for lunch, as he did every other day. Bell stayed behind with the Kid and played cards.

With only himself and Bell in the building, the Kid asked to be taken to the privy out back. Bell obliged. Many historians believe someone had hidden a gun in the privy intended for the Kid's use. Others disagree, but nevertheless, when the Kid returned and entered the building ready to go up the stairs to his cell, he bolted up the narrow steps, far ahead of the deputy. He stopped on the second-floor landing, pulled one hand out of the heavy iron handcuff, and, as Bell neared, the Kid swung the metal, striking Bell on the side of his head (autopsy reports confirmed this). Then the Kid grabbed a pistol and fired. Bell stumbled down the stairs and lurched outside to the corral. He fell dead before reaching the gate.

The Kid rushed to the armory across the hall from his cell and grabbed Olinger's shotgun.

Hearing a gunshot, Olinger left his prisoners at the Wortley Hotel dining room. He assumed Bell had shot the Kid—something he'd wanted to do himself—and he rushed toward the courthouse.

The Kid pushed open the wooden window frame from his second-floor cell, leaned out, and pressed Olinger's fully loaded shotgun to his shoulder. He gazed down at the deputy directly under his window and called out, "Hello, old boy."

When Olinger looked up, the Kid unloaded both barrels. Olinger fell dead, his shoulders and chest riddled. He had just turned thirty-one.

His mother, Rebecca Olinger, said this about her son: "Bob was a murderer from the cradle, and if there is a hell hereafter, then he is there."[14]

Later, the Kid remarked about shooting James Bell. "I did not want to kill Bell, but I had to do so in order to save my own life. It was a case of have to, not wanting to."

With shackles on his legs, the Kid hopped downstairs and out to the back. Blacksmith Godfrey Gauss, Tunstall's former cook and a friend of the Kid, cut through the iron shackles so that he

This upper-story courthouse window is where Billy leaned out and shot
Olinger. A stone marker where Olinger died is at the base of the building.
MYKE GROVES

was able to mount a horse. He grabbed reins, but the mare wasn't happy having him and the iron on his back and immediately bucked him off. The Kid rolled into the street. Undaunted, the Kid tucked up both shackles under his belt. Locals, now gathered around, urged him on. The county clerk offered his horse, and the Kid swung up into the saddle with no problem. Now successfully mounted and not in a huge hurry—after all, there was *no* law in town—he trotted out of town almost an hour after killing the deputies. Several people stood watching him leave and waved adios.

ON THE LAM

After escaping from jail, Billy spent the next ten weeks looking over his shoulder, constantly wondering when Garrett or a bounty hunter would appear. With $500 ($13,300 today) on his head, he would be worth the trouble of catching. He moved from sheep camp to sheep camp, enjoying true friendship and hospitality but returning frequently to Fort Sumner. El Chivato (the Infant Rascal), as he was affectionately called, often dressed as a herder.

Most everyone urged him to head for Mexico, where he'd be safe from the long arm of the law. Besides, they said, the Kid spoke Spanish better than some of the native speakers and he knew many of their customs. He'd be safe there.

But no. The need to belong kept him near Lincoln, the town filled with Hispanics and Irish—the combination he closely identified with. Not only that, but Fort Sumner was where Paulita Maxwell, his latest *novia*, lived. Although Paulita later denied a romance, there is no doubt she was one of Billy's favorites. Many who knew the Kid believed it was his deep love for Paulita that kept him in Fort Sumner. Historian Frederick Nolan theorized that Sheriff Pat Garrett, whose wife was sister to one of the Kid's girlfriends, Celsa, had heard the women speak of Paulita's pregnancy.

If indeed the Kid fathered several children, it is no wonder there are no official records. Society of the day frowned on having children out of wedlock, and especially for Paulita, it would have been devastating for the family to admit to such an alliance. After all, the Maxwells were the owners of one of the largest ranches in the territory, and they wielded much power. As the Kid's mother had experienced, wealthy families wanted nothing to do with scandal.

Surely, Paulita had told the Kid (or maybe he guessed) of her pregnancy shortly before his arrest at Stinking Springs in December 1880. If true, logically, that was the reason Billy stayed around Fort Sumner and the reason he was still there when he was killed.

Nine days after his escape from Lincoln, the Kid made his way to the fort.

If gossip around Fort Sumner was correct that seventeen-year-old Paulita was pregnant with Billy's child, this was exactly what he had longed for—a wife, children, and a home. He had to remain by her side. More gossip revealed that Billy and Paulita were planning to elope to Mexico, where they'd buy a ranch and have many more *niños*.

Becoming a "Bonnie Lass Toolie"

According to some stories, the Kid even resorted to dressing like a woman to evade capture. According to Billy's friend Jesus Silva in a 1936 interview, Silva found the fugitive Kid walking in leg irons along the road eight miles south of Fort Sumner. At some point, his horse had thrown him and had returned to Lincoln. Silva rescued the Kid and left him at the home of Jesus Anaya.

"Anaya had three daughters, and when strangers would come, [the Kid] dressed up like a girl and stayed in the kitchen with the Anaya girls. And he made a good one, too—

he was small, his hair was long, and he talked Mexican just as good as them."[15]

A man of many talents, the Kid had indeed become a good-looking woman, a "bonnie lass toolie."

BLACK CLOUDS LOOMING

If subterfuge had worked once for Pat Garrett in December when he tricked the Kid and his gang into coming to Bowdre's house (where Tom Folliard was killed), surely it would work again. Garrett spread the word that he and his deputies were nowhere near Fort Sumner, supposedly out chasing the Kid toward the southern part of the state when, in fact, they were in town. Sheriff Garrett had brought along Panhandle Stock Association detective John Poe, a former town and Texas U.S. marshal, and Deputy Kip McKinney, neither of whom knew what the Kid looked like. They waited in a peach orchard not far from Pete Maxwell's house.

The three lawmen crept toward the Fort Sumner buildings but stopped when they heard other voices in the orchard. They spotted a man who had been crouching and watched as he stood. Although the man was in full view, he was too far away to be identified. In silhouette, the man wore a broad-brimmed hat and a dark vest and pants and was in shirtsleeves. Was it Billy perhaps?

Although it was a waning moon, illumination high at 80 percent, Garrett was unable to be sure who they were looking at. The dark figure mumbled something soft, jumped the fence, and walked into the compound. Garrett and his deputies backed out of the orchard. Poe sat on the edge of Maxwell's south porch steps, and McKinney squatted outside an open gate nearby.

Close to midnight, Garrett slipped into Pete's bedroom and shook his shoulder. Figuring Pete Maxwell, the largest landowner in that part of the state, must know of Billy's whereabouts, he softly asked what he knew. Pete was a wealthy and influential person in the community, and since the Kid had a reputation as quite the lady's man, Pete didn't like the idea of his sister being courted by an outlaw no matter how much he actually liked him. In fact, he'd heard rumors that Paulita was pregnant with the Kid's child. That could never be.

The Kid, tired from worrying that he'd be arrested but anticipating a loving night with Paulita, had followed the cottonwoods along the Pecos River, through the peach orchard, and to the side yard of the Maxwell's long, low adobe house. He quietly entered and made his way straight to Paulita's bedroom on the southeast corner. Spotting her snuggled in bed, he began to undress—laying his pistol on a nearby table, taking off his vest, pulling off his boots—but quickly realized something wasn't right. Movement outside the window on the old parade ground startled him. Heart pounding, he ducked under the window, then carefully peeked out. Two men crouched near the front gate, both speaking quietly. Who were they? No one he knew. Something was definitely amiss.

If anyone knew what was going on, it would be Paulita's brother Pete, whose bedroom was across the hall. Senses on high alert, the Kid left his gun on the table, tiptoed out of Paulita's room, and crept across the corridor to Pete's room. Although it was dark, from the doorway he recognized Pete's figure lying in bed. He backed into the room and whispered, "*¿Pedro, quiénes son esos hombres afuera?*" (Pete, who are those men outside?)

Pete whispered to Garrett, "*El es.*" (It's him.)

At the same time, the Kid realized someone else was in the room. His heart pounded, but he froze. "*¿Quien es?*" (Who is it?), he asked, then repeated, "*¿Quien es?*"

Surprised that the Kid had walked into his arms, literally, Garrett pulled stealthily at his holstered gun. He had one problem—he was sitting on his holster, and standing to straighten and pull the gun was no option. The six-foot-four Garrett was easy to identify. The Kid would recognize him instantly and bolt. Garrett worked the leather around while he held his breath in the darkness. Finally, Garrett freed his gun and fired twice. The first bullet struck the Kid in the chest, and the second ricocheted off a nightstand. The Kid spun and crumpled to the wooden floor.

Like cowards, Garrett and Pete Maxwell bolted out a door and into another room.

Billy the Kid let out his final breath. He was barely twenty.

CHAPTER THIRTEEN

THE REST OF THE STORY

"Always the Mexican people had looked forward to Billy's coming. They would say 'We love Billicito . . . we make a fiesta.'"

—EVE BALL, AUTHOR OF *MA'AM JONES OF THE PECOS*

SO MANY CHARACTERS WERE INTRINSIC TO THE MAKING OF Billy the Kid, at times it's hard to keep them straight. What happened to them? Did they ride off into history or make a name for themselves? Were they themselves shot down in the prime of life or did they live to a ripe old age?

In alphabetical order, here are some of the main players of Billy's story.

BILL ANTRIM, BILLY'S STEPFATHER
An expert on recognizing and extracting silver, Bill Antrim examined ore samples and pronounced the claim's worth. His life centered around mining. He was reported to have lived in the mining towns of Graham (1898), Cooney (1904), and Mogollon (1906). In 1912, he returned to Mogollon, New Mexico.

A friend of Antrim living in Mogollon reported that Antrim had begun to find the winters there in the mountains too cold. Since Antrim had an income from property he still owned in

Kansas, he no longer had to work. Around 1914, he started spending winters in much warmer El Paso. Reportedly, in 1918 he was living in a rooming house on North Stanton Street in El Paso.

Antrim moved to Adelaida, California to be closer to his niece. He died December 10, 1922, at eighty years old. Ironically, he never spoke of or wrote about his stepson who had become a legend.

JOSEPH "JOSIE" BONNEY MCCARTY ANTRIM, BILLY'S YOUNGER BROTHER

A card dealer like his brother, Joseph was also a runner for poker games all his adult life, becoming a drifter as well as an opium addict, an alcoholic, a gambler, a miner, a room clerk, and a day laborer. At one point, he met Pat Garrett, either in Trinidad, Colorado, or Albuquerque, New Mexico. After a long conversation in which no one knows exactly what was said, they shook hands and went separate ways. Joseph was also a cook in an Albuquerque hotel in 1883 (which would have been a convenient place to meet Garrett) and a bartender in El Paso, Texas, before wandering up to Den-

Joseph Bonney Antrim in his later years. He was a teenager the last time he saw older brother Billy. AUTHOR'S COLLECTION

ver. Along the way, he fathered a child and then married.

In 1928, journalist Ed Hoover of the *Denver Post* interviewed Joseph, an "old-timer," widely known as a gambler in his day, who had become penniless. When the article came out, someone pointed out to Hoover that Joseph Antrim was Billy the Kid's brother.

Hoover replied, "So what?" Many aficionados and historians would love to have taken that reporter's place (or shaken him violently).

He did add, however, that Joseph was rather colorless. During this interview, Joseph mentioned that his brother, mother, and father (presumably Bill Antrim) had moved to Denver when he was young. He also reported that Antrim was a Wells Fargo Express agent. Considering Antrim had been a teamster in Indiana, his being employed as an express agent was logical.

Joseph died on November 25, 1930, taking all the family history to his grave. When no one claimed his body, it was donated to the Colorado Medical School.

SUSAN MCSWEEN BARBER, WIDOW OF LAWYER ALEXANDER MCSWEEN

A powerhouse of a woman aptly termed the "Cattle Queen of New Mexico," Susan McSween served as executor of her husband's estate along with that of John Tunstall. John Chisum gifted her forty head of cattle, and she began a cattle empire, eventually running more than 8,000 head. She married George Barber in 1880, and by 1890, her ranch holdings were some of the largest in the territory. She became extremely wealthy through cattle sales and silver mining on the property.

Susan McSween Barber was a feisty woman who sued the U.S. government over the death of her husband (she lost), then became a cattle baron in her own right. She settled in White Oaks, New Mexico, later in life.
AUTHOR'S COLLECTION

In 1902, she sold most of her holdings and moved to White Oaks, New Mexico. She died there in 1931 at age eighty-five.

FRANK COE, CLOSE FRIEND OF BILLY

After the Lincoln County War ended, Frank Coe left New Mexico, living for a time in Colorado and Nebraska. In Colorado, he'd been arrested for the murder of Buckshot Roberts. However, further inspection revealed it was Frank's cousin George who'd done the shooting. In 1884, Frank returned to Lincoln County, bought a ranch, and lived out his life there. In 1880, Frank was suspected of taking part in another lynching but was never charged. He and his wife, Helena Anne Tully, lived together for fifty years and raised six children. He died in 1931 at age seventy-nine.

GEORGE COE, ANOTHER CLOSE FRIEND OF BILLY

George, Frank's cousin, enjoyed showing off his wound (he lost a finger) from the gunfight at Blazer's Mill. Eventually, George

This rare photo of George Coe shows him at the site of John Tunstall's murder.
COURTESY OF TARA WOODRUFF, GREAT-GREAT-GRANDDAUGHTER OF GEORGE COE

was granted amnesty by New Mexico Governor Lew Wallace. In 1884, he started the Golden Glow Ranch in Lincoln County and became a prosperous and respected member of the community.

George wrote his autobiography, *Frontier Fighter*, in which he explained his association with the Regulators and gave details of certain members' traits and personalities. He died on November 12, 1941, in Roswell, New Mexico.

JIMMY DOLAN, CENTER OF THE LINCOLN COUNTY WAR

Born in Ireland, James Joseph Dolan served two years in the U.S. Army. In May 1873, Dolan attempted to shoot a U.S. cavalry captain at Fort Stanton, resulting in L. G. Murphy & Co. being evicted from the fort.

Dolan committed only one murder with his own hands; he preferred to direct others to commit such acts on his behalf. A close ally of the Ring, Dolan was at the center of the Lincoln County War. Although suffering from alcoholism, he served as the Lincoln County treasurer and in the territorial senate. He died on his ranch in 1898, aged forty-nine, having finally acquired all of Tunstall's property. Later, much of the land was seized by the federal government as part of land conservation with the remainder being sold off.

TOM O. FOLLIARD, BILLY'S BEST FRIEND

Around the late 1850s, Tom's father, also Thomas O. Folliard, emigrated to the United States from Ireland, and he met and married Sarah Cook. Two years later, they had a son, Tom. Following the Civil War, the elder Folliard moved the family to Monclova in the Mexican state of Coahuila. There, Tom Sr. and Sarah fell victims of smallpox and died. Tom, a baby, was taken in by a native family and raised until such time as members of his own family could retrieve him.

John Cook, Sarah's uncle, took young Tom back to his home in Uvalde, Texas. The Uvalde census of 1870 lists "Thomas Folliard, 9 years old." Others in the household included David and Eliza Jane Cook, Tom's grandparents. (His name is often noted as Tom O'Folliard, his middle initial used as the beginning of his last name. The correct spelling is Folliard.) Tom rode with the Kid through thick and thin until his own untimely death on December 17, 1880, at Fort Sumner, when he was shot by Sheriff Pat Garrett, who had mistaken Tom for Billy. He is buried next to Billy in the Fort Sumner Cemetery.

PAT GARRETT, THE MAN WHO KILLED BILLY THE KID

Patrick Floyd Garrett, former buffalo hunter and cattle rustler, was elected Lincoln County sheriff precisely because he was friends with Billy the Kid. On January 14, 1880, Garrett married Apolinaria Gutierrez, and between 1881 and 1905, she gave birth to eight children: Ida (who died in 1896), Dudley, Elizabeth, Annie, Patrick, Pauline, Oscar, and Jarvis.

After killing Billy, twice Pat Garrett set up schemes to get investors to fund a company that would irrigate the desert in an area with bad soil and no water. The second company he helped found eventually fired him. He held various jobs, always in financial debt. Somehow, he went on to be nominated by President Theodore Roosevelt in 1901 as collector of customs in El Paso, Texas. Garrett's lack of diplomacy resulted in a fistfight with a former employee and accusations of "gross neglect and suspicious dealing." When his term ended, he was not reappointed.

Even though he killed the legendary outlaw, Garrett didn't capitalize on his fame, never becoming the celebrated figure he thought he should be. Ranching bored him, and he was surly, too much so for politics. Even his friends called him "one of the meanest sons-of-bitches around." He drank heavily and accumulated massive debts.

"Garrett was an overrated man," said Frank Coe. "At Fort Sumner he stole many bull teams and sold them to butchers at Las Vegas, New Mexico. His killings of Charlie Bowdre, Tom O. Folliard and Billy the Kid were little short of deliberate, premediated murders."[1]

Garrett returned to his ranch twenty-five miles east of Las Cruces, where he speculated in mining, tried to practice law in Mexico, but mainly drank and was crochety. At one point, he left his family in Las Cruces and moved to El Paso, where he lived with a known prostitute, "Mrs. Brown."

In the end, he had as many enemies as friends.

One of history's oddest assassinations claimed Garrett. On February 29, 1908, he rode in a buckboard with Carl Adamson and Garrett's son-in-law from his ranch on the way to Las Cruces. Here, he and Adamson encountered a group of riders, among them a twenty-one-year-old cowboy, Wayne Brazel, who was running goats on Garrett's land. The two argued.

"They halted near Alameda Arroyo. While Garrett stood at the rear of the wagon, removed his left glove, and unbuttoned his trousers to relieve himself, one bullet tore through the back of his head and a second entered his stomach."[2] One of the other men said Garrett fell like a sack of potatoes.

His killer has never been officially identified, although Brazel confessed, calling it self-defense. In the 1909 trial, Brazel was defended by Albert Fall (of the Teapot Dome scandal). The prosecution wondered how a man could urinate and pose a threat at the same time. Nevertheless, Brazel was acquitted.

Garrett's daughter, Elizabeth, wrote the New Mexico state song, "O Fair New Mexico," in 1917.

ALEXANDER GRZELACHOWSKI, PUERTO DE LUNA MERCANTILE OWNER

In 1862, Alexander Grzelachowski joined the New Mexico Volunteers as a chaplain. After his short service, he left the priesthood and went into the mercantile business in Las Vegas, New Mexico. He started a family in 1870 and by 1872 had moved to Puerto de Luna, where he opened a mercantile store forty miles up the Pecos River from Fort Sumner.

People called him "Padre Polaco" (Polish Padre). The jovial storekeeper not only provided supplies for the area but also ran cattle on the grassy plains east of Fort Sumner. Billy stopped there often and even attended dances the Padre sponsored. When Billy would come by, Grzelachowski allowed the young outlaw to take whatever supplies he needed, though Billy was known to have rustled horses from Grzelachowski's ranches.

Quite active in civil affairs, in 1891, Grzelachowski played an influential role in lobbying the territorial legislature for the creation of a new county out of the southern part of San Miguel County. Guadalupe County was officially created in 1893 with Grzelachowski serving as the new county's first probate judge. As postmaster for Puerto de Luna, he operated the post office out of his mercantile store. In addition, he ranched and raised sheep, cattle, and horses.

The Polish Padre died in 1896 of injuries suffered when he was thrown from a wagon.

JOHN KINNEY, LEADER OF THE BANDITTI OF NEW MEXICO

In true western fashion, John Kinney went from being a leader of a rustling/killing gang to deputy sheriff and then back to rustling.

Kinney's brutal gang, along with the newly formed Jesse Evans gang, was enlisted by the Murphy-Dolan faction at the outset of the Lincoln County War. To counter Billy and his Regulators, Sheriff George Peppin deputized Kinney. This gave Kinney's gang legal freedom to run rampant in the county. During the siege of the McSween house, Billy fired a shot, hitting Kinney in the face, and Billy's leg was grazed. The deputy survived. In 1878, Kinney was arrested for murder but was acquitted.

Arrested for cattle rustling in 1883, Kinney was sentenced to prison. Released after three years, he did not return to outlaw life. He served in the U.S. Army during the Spanish-American War and was a successful Arizona miner before retiring to Prescott, Arizona, to live with a daughter. He died on August 25, 1919.

PAULITA MAXWELL, BILLY'S NOVIA

Denying in later years she'd been the love of Billy the Kid, Paulita claimed Billy had liked Celsa Gutierrez better. Shortly after Billy's death, Paulita met José Jaramillo, a man she barely knew. They courted, and she gave birth to a daughter. Rumors abounded that the girl was the Kid's, but Paulita never said.

In 1883, she officially married José, and together they had two more children. A few years later, she divorced José for his infidelity. Paulita died in 1930 at Fort Sumner at age sixty-five. She is buried in the military cemetery not far from Billy.

PETE MAXWELL, BILLY'S FRIEND AND BETRAYER

Pete Maxwell lived in his father's shadow his entire life, never achieving the status that father Lucien Maxwell enjoyed. Lucien Maxwell had founded the town of Cimarron, New Mexico, and made his home there, where Pete was born in 1848. When Fort Sumner was abandoned by the U.S. Army, Lucien purchased the site and made major improvements not only to the housing quarters and buildings but also the area around it. He planted orchards and raised cattle. Lucien moved there with his family in 1871.

Following Lucien's death in 1875, Pete took over managing the business. Pete was a friend of Billy and yet not supportive when the outlaw came to court Paulita. Despite being a wealthy landowner and influential man in the territory, Pete would spend the rest of his days trying to live down what happened immediately after Garrett shot Billy. Garrett fired the second shot, and both Pete and Garrett bolted from the room, huddling somewhere in the dark house. It was Deluvina Maxwell, the Navajo housekeeper, who bravely entered the smoke-filled room to find Billy dead on the floor. She was devastated. But she confirmed that Billy wore no boots and carried no weapon.

Pete's act of running away labeled him a coward for the rest of his days. The locals referred to him as "Don Chootme." Pete died at Fort Sumner on June 21, 1898.

Maxwell House, Focal Point of Fort Sumner

Pete Maxwell's former Fort Sumner dwelling was a long, one-story building, consistent with many military post buildings of the time. One of the officers' quarters became the Maxwell home. Pete's bedroom on the corner was across the hall from Paulita's.

In the days before air conditioning, windows (but never doors) were wide open, allowing breezes to cool a room. Oriented northeast to southwest, the Maxwell house had plenty

Pete Maxwell's house in Fort Sumner, where Billy was shot by Sheriff Pat Garrett.
COURTESY OF PALACE OF THE GOVERNORS, NEGATIVE #045559

of doors and windows. Pete Maxwell's bedroom, according to the army floor plan, had four windows: two on the northwest side and two on the southwest side. Since it was July and quite warm, even at night, it is logical to assume that at least one and probably all the windows were open. The door, however, would have been closed because nocturnal creatures, such as skunks, will walk boldly into a house through an open door.

"In the mid-1890s, the New England Livestock Co. had liquidated its cattle interests and piecemeal sold off the land within the vast Fort Sumner ranch. In the process, one of the owners tore down the old Maxwell house, salvaged the lumber and used it in the building of a ranch house thirty miles east on the Llano Estacado."[3]

One by one, the vacant adobe buildings of the fort fell into ruin. Members of Lucien Maxwell's original colony, many of them friends of Billy, were now dispersed. Some moved to new communities in the area, while others left the territory. The ruins were washed away in the 1937 Pecos River floods.

LAWRENCE MURPHY, CENTER OF LINCOLN COUNTY WAR

Born in County Wexford, Ireland, Lawrence Murphy moved to the United States as an adult. In 1851, he enlisted in the U.S. Army. After being discharged in 1861, he ventured to Santa Fe and reenlisted once again in the Union army. He served for the duration of the Civil War but saw little if any combat. He mustered out at Fort Stanton in 1866.

Although suffering from cancer and alcoholism, Murphy was a main instigator of the Lincoln County War. However, because he was not well, he had little to do with the day-to-day activities of his businesses or the gunmen under his employ. He died on October 20, 1878, around the age of forty-seven.

"DIRTY" DAVE RUDABAUGH, PARTNERED WITH BILLY

After being captured by Pat Garrett at Stinking Springs, Rudabaugh, shackled with Billy, was returned to Las Vegas and then to Santa Fe, where he stood trial and was found guilty of murdering a Las Vegas deputy. Sentenced to life in prison, he escaped and fled to Arizona, where he joined Ike Clanton and his gang. He may have participated in the murder of Morgan Earp.

When the Clanton gang broke up, Rudabaugh rode down to Mexico working as both a cowboy and a rustler.

On February 18, 1886, Rudabaugh was involved in a gunfight over a card game with locals in Parral, Chihuahua. He killed two men and wounded another. He left the saloon unscathed but could not find his horse. He reentered a few moments later and was shot several times from the shadows. He was then decapitated, and his head was placed on a pole.

YGINIO SALAZAR, PAL OF BILLY THE KID

A close friend of Billy and about his age, Salazar fought in the Five-Day Battle and was one of fourteen Regulators inside McSween's house. Along with others, fifteen-year-old Yginio Salazar bolted outside, fleeing the burning home. He was shot in the back and shoulder. Pretending to be dead so as not to be shot again, he lay still until the fighting was over. Then he crawled half a mile to his sister-in-law's house and was treated by the doctor at Fort Stanton. Salazar later became a rancher. After Billy escaped from jail in Lincoln, he fled to Salazar's home and camped nearby. Salazar brought him food and water.

Salazar continued farming in the nearby small community of Las Tablas and remained a close friend of Billy. He died of natural causes in 1936 and was buried in Lincoln's cemetery beside his wife, who died in 1935. His headstone reads "Pal of Billy the Kid."

LEW WALLACE, NEW MEXICO TERRITORY GOVERNOR

Selected by President Rutherford B. Hayes to serve as the governor of the New Mexico Territory in 1878, Wallace was tasked with putting an end to the Lincoln County turmoil and controlling the Indian uprisings. He managed to find time to write *Ben Hur*, and his wife Susan wrote *Land of the Pueblos*. Not only a writer but also an artist, Lew contributed a pencil drawing to Susan's book, and he enjoyed time painting in oils in the secluded alleys behind the Palace of the Governors in Santa Fe.

Neither he nor his wife, Susan, much liked New Mexico. Susan wrote a letter to her son, Henry Lane Wallace, in which she said, "We should have another war with Old Mexico and make her take back New Mexico. I did not believe anything could cause me to think well of Santa Fe, but this hideous spot, Fort Stanton, does." Lew stated, "Every calculation based on experience elsewhere fails in New Mexico."[4]

After New Mexico, he went on to serve as U.S. minister to the Ottoman Empire (1881–1885). Wallace retired to his home in Crawfordsville, Indiana, where he continued to write until his death in 1905.

NOTES

INTRODUCTION
1. *La Colombe* [*The Dove*], Spanish words, anonymous English words, anonymous music, Sebastian Yradier, G. Schirmer, copyright 1877. (Published earlier in Paris by Au Ménestrel [Henri Heugel].)
2. "Patrick's Day Parade," written by Edward Harrigan, music by David Braham, Wm. A. Pond & Co., copyright 1874.
3. Robert M. Utley, *Billy the Kid: A Short and Violent Life* (Lincoln: University of Nebraska Press, 1989), 1.
4. Jerry Weddle, *Antrim Is My Stepfather's Name: The Childhood of Billy the Kid* (Tucson: Arizona Historical Society, 1993), xv.
5. Ibid., xvi.
6. Richard W. Etulain and Glenda Riley, *With Badges and Bullets: Lawmen and Outlaws in the Old West* (Golden, CO: Fulcrum Publishing, 1999), 123.

CHAPTER ONE
1. Ralph Estes, *The Autobiography of Billy the Kid* (n.p.: Black Rose Writing, 2012), 13.
2. W. C. Jameson, *Billy the Kid: Investigating History's Mysteries* (Lanham, MD: TwoDot, 2018), 53.
3. Michael Wallis, *Billy the Kid: The Endless Ride* (New York: Norton, 2007), 6.
4. Jerry Weddle, *Antrim Is My Stepfather's Name: The Childhood of Billy the Kid* (Tucson: Arizona Historical Society, 1993), 7–8.
5. Ibid., 8.
6. Bob Boze Bell, *Billy the Kid: The Final Word* (Cave Creek, AZ: Two Roads West, 2021), 2.

CHAPTER TWO
1. Don Cline, *Antrim and Billy* (College Station, TX: Creative Publishing, 1990), 26.

2. Michael Wallis, *Billy the Kid: The Endless Ride* (New York: Norton, 2007), 23.

3. Ibid., 20.

4. Allen Barra, *Inventing Wyatt Earp* (New York: Carroll & Graf, 1998), 37.

5. Wallis, *Billy the Kid*, 20.

6. Ibid., 35

7. Ibid., 23.

8. Ibid., 37.

CHAPTER THREE

1. Candy Moulton, trails historian, WWA Executive Director interview, February 2021.

2. Bob Boze Bell, *Billy the Kid: The Final Word* (Cave Creek, AZ: Two Roads West, 2021), 4.

3. Michael Wallis, *Billy the Kid: The Endless Ride* (New York: Norton, 2007), 4.

4. Lynn Michelson, *Billy the Kid in Santa Fe* (Santa Fe, NM: Cleanan Press, 2019), 41.

5. Wallis, *Billy the Kid*, 53.

CHAPTER FOUR

1. Jerry Weddle, *Antrim Is My Stepfather's Name: The Childhood of Billy the Kid* (Tucson, Arizona Historical Society, 1993), 4.

2. Patrick F. Garrett, *The Authentic Life of Billy, the Kid* (Norman: University of Oklahoma Press, 1954), 9.

3. Michael Wallis, *Billy the Kid: The Endless Ride* (New York: Norton, 2007), 75.

4. Weddle, *Antrim Is My Stepfather's Name*, 7.

5. Robert M. Utley, *Billy the Kid: A Short and Violent Life* (Lincoln: University of Nebraska Press, 1989), 7.

6. Weddle, *Antrim Is My Stepfather's Name*, 8.

7. Utley, *Billy the Kid*, 7.

8. Richard W. Etulain and Glenda Riley, eds., *With Badges and Bullets: Lawmen and Outlaws in the Old West* (Golden, CO: Fulcrum Publishing, 1999), 124.

9. Utley, *Billy the Kid*, 7.

10. Weddle, *Antrim Is My Stepfather's Name*, 30.

11. Don Cline, *Antrim and Billy* (College Station, TX: Creative Publishing, 1990), 96.

CHAPTER FIVE

1. Robert M. Utley, *Billy the Kid: A Short and Violent Life* (Lincoln: University of Nebraska Press, 1898), 7.

2. Jerry Weddle, *Antrim Is My Stepfather's Name: The Childhood of Billy the Kid* (Tucson, Arizona Historical Society, 1993), 24.
3. *Miners Life* newspaper article, September 23, 1875.
4. Weddle, *Antrim Is My Stepfather's Name*, 24.
5. Michael Wallis, *Billy the Kid: The Endless Ride* (New York: Norton, 2007), 88.
6. Weddle, *Antrim Is My Stepfather's Name*, 26.
7. Richard Etulain, *Thunder in the West* (Norman: University of Oklahoma Press, 2020), 35.
8. Bob Boze Bell, *Billy the Kid: The Final Word* (Cave Creek, AZ: Two Roads West, 2021), 8.
9. Weddle, *Antrim Is My Stepfather's Name*, 27.
10. Wallis, *Billy the Kid*, 89.
11. Weddle, *Antrim Is My Stepfather's Name*, 28.

CHAPTER SIX

1. Jerry Weddle, *Antrim Is My Stepfather's Name: The Childhood of Billy the Kid* (Tucson: Arizona Historical Society, 1993), 31.
2. Ibid., 33.
3. Ibid., 34.
4. Ibid.
5. Ibid., 41.
6. Ibid.
7. Danny Haralson, "Did You Know . . . What Fort Grant Dragged In with It, Part 2," *Eastern Arizona Courier*, June 19, 2016.
8. Mark Lee Gardner, *To Hell on a Fast Horse* (New York: William Morrow, 2010), 47.
9. Weddle, *Antrim Is My Stepfather's Name*, 42.
10. Sam Lowe, *Jerks in New Mexico History* (Guilford, CT: Morris Book Publishing, 2012), 4.
11. Michael Wallis, *Billy the Kid: The Endless Ride* (New York: Norton, 2007), 115.

CHAPTER SEVEN

1. Robert M. Utley, *Billy the Kid: A Short and Violent Life* (Lincoln: University of Nebraska Press, 1898), 13.
2. Jerry Weddle, *Antrim Is My Stepfather's Name: The Childhood of Billy the Kid* (Tucson: Arizona Historical Society, 1993), 46.
3. Michael Wallis, *Billy the Kid: The Endless Ride* (New York: Norton, 2007), 128.
4. Ibid., 130.
5. Ibid., 136.

6. Eve Ball, *Ma'am Jones of the Pecos* (Tucson: University of Arizona Press, 1969), 117.

7. Bob Boze Bell, *Billy the Kid: The Final Word* (Cave Creek, AZ: Two Roads West, 2021), 19.

CHAPTER EIGHT

1. Michael Wallis, *Billy the Kid: The Endless Ride* (New York: Norton, 2007), 194.

2. Ibid., 146.

3. Miguel Antonio Otero, *The Real Billy the Kid with New Light on the Lincoln County War* (Santa Fe, NM: Sunstone Press, 2007), 145.

4. Richard W. Etulain, *Thunder in the West* (Norman: University of Oklahoma Press, 2020), 57.

5. Ray John de Aragón, *Billy the Kid Meets His Ghost* (Albuquerque, NM: Event Horizon Press, 2015), 16.

6. Ibid.

7. Ibid., 13.

8. Otero, *The Real Billy the Kid with New Light on the Lincoln County War*, 147.

9. Eve Ball, *Ma'am Jones of the Pecos* (Tucson: University of Arizona Press, 1969), 120.

10. Wallis, *Billy the Kid*, 196.

11. Ibid., 195.

12. Otero, *The Real Billy the Kid with New Light on the Lincoln County War*, 136.

13. Robert M. Utley., *Billy the Kid, a Short and Violent Life* (Lincoln: University of Nebraska Press, 1898), 48.

CHAPTER NINE

1. Richard W. Etulain, *Thunder in the West* (Norman: University of Oklahoma Press, 2020), 94.

2. Bob Boze Bell, *Billy the Kid: The Final Word* (Cave Creek, AZ: Two Roads West, 2021), 29.

3. Michael Wallis, *Billy the Kid: The Endless Ride* (New York: Norton, 2007), 203.

4. Bell, *Billy the Kid*, 41.

5. Ibid., 48.

6. Ibid., 51.

7. Wallis, *Billy the Kid*, 223.

8. Bell, *Billy the Kid*, 52.

9. Ibid.

10. James H. Earl, ed., *The Capture of Billy the Kid* (College Station, TX: Creative Publishing, 1988), 50

CHAPTER TEN

1. Johnny D. Boggs, *Billy the Kid on Film, 1911–2012* (Jefferson, NC: McFarland, 2013), 9.
2. Michael Wallis, *Billy the Kid: The Endless Ride* (New York: Norton, 2007), 227.
3. Robert M. Utley, *Billy the Kid: A Short and Violent Life* (Lincoln: University of Nebraska Press, 1898), 119.
4. Bob Boze Bell, *Billy the Kid: The Final Word* (Cave Creek, AZ: Two Roads West, 2021), 66.
5. Ibid., 61.

CHAPTER ELEVEN

1. Robert M. Utley, *Billy the Kid: A Short and Violent Life* (Lincoln: University of Nebraska Press, 1898), 145.
2. Richard W. Etulain and Glenda Riley, eds., *With Badges and Bullets: Lawmen and Outlaws in the Old West* (Golden, CO: Fulcrum Publishing, 1999), 134.
3. Marc Simmons, *Stalking Billy the Kid: Brief Sketches of a Short Life* (Santa Fe, NM: Sunstone Press, 2006), 111.
4. James H. Earle, ed., *The Capture of Billy the Kid* (College Station, TX: Creative Publishing, 1988), 124.
5. Bob Boze Bell, *Billy the Kid: The Final Word* (Cave Creek, AZ: Two Roads West, 2021), 99.
6. Earle, *The Capture of Billy the Kid*, 140–41; *Las Vegas Gazette*, December 28, 1880.
7. W. C. Jameson, *Billy the Kid: Investigating History's Mysteries* (Lanham, MD: TwoDot, 2018), 92–93.
8. Bell, *Billy the Kid*, 102.

CHAPTER TWELVE

1. Bob Boze Bell, *Billy the Kid: The Final Word* (Cave Creek, AZ: Two Roads West, 2021), 104.
2. Ibid., 105.
3. Ibid., 104.
4. Marc Simmons, *Stalking Billy the Kid: Brief Sketches of a Short Life* (Santa Fe, NM: Sunstone Press, 2006), 107.
5. Bell, *Billy the Kid*, 105.
6. Ibid., 107.
7. Simmons, *Stalking Billy the Kid*, 70.
8. Jon Tuska, *Billy the Kid: His Life and Legend* (Albuquerque: University of New Mexico Press, 1994), 96.
9. Ibid.
10. Bell, *Billy the Kid*, 109.

11. Ibid.

12. Melody Groves, *When Outlaws Wore Badges* (Lanham, MD: TwoDot, 2021), 110.

13. Ibid., 112.

14. Ibid., 105.

15. Jesus Silva, *Amarillo Daily News*, November 13, 1936.

CHAPTER THIRTEEN

1. Miguel Antonio Otero, *The Real Billy the Kid with New Light on the Lincoln County War* (Santa Fe, NM: Sunstone Press, 2007), 144.

2. Richard W. Etulain and Glenda Riley, eds., *With Badges and Bullets: Lawmen and Outlaws in the Old West* (Golden, CO: Fulcrum Publishing, 1999), 67.

3. W. C. Jameson, *Billy the Kid: Investigating History's Mysteries* (Lanham, MD: TwoDot, 2018), 138.

4. Marc Simmons, "Trail Dust: Lew Wallace and Wife Found Early New Mexico Primitive," *The New Mexican*, March 15, 2013.

BIBLIOGRAPHY

Ball, Eve. *Ma'am Jones of the Pecos*. Tucson: University of Arizona Press, 1969.

Barra, Allen. *Inventing Wyatt Earp*. New York: Carroll & Graf, 1998.

Bell, Bob Boze. *Billy the Kid: The Final Word*. Cave Creek, AZ: Two Roads West, 2021.

Boggs, Johnny D. *Billy the Kid on Film, 1911–2012*. Jefferson, NC: McFarland, 2013.

Cline, Don. *Antrim and Billy*. College Station, TX: Creative Publishing, 1990.

de Aragón, Ray John. *Billy the Kid Meets His Ghost*. Albuquerque, NM: Event Horizon Press, 2015.

Earle, James H., ed. *The Capture of Billy the Kid*. College Station, TX: Creative Publishing, 1988.

Estes, Ralph. *The Autobiography of Billy the Kid*. N.p.: Black Rose Writing, 2012.

Etulain, Richard W. *Thunder in the West*. Norman: University of Oklahoma Press, 2020.

Etulain, Richard W., and Glenda Riley, eds. *With Badges and Bullets: Lawmen and Outlaws in the Old West*. Golden, CO: Fulcrum Publishing, 1999.

Gardner, Mark Lee. *To Hell on a Fast Horse*. New York: HarperCollins, 2010.

Garrett, Patrick F. *The Authentic Life of Billy, the Kid*. Norman: University of Oklahoma Press, 1954.

Groves, Melody. *When Outlaws Wore Badges*. Lanham, MD: TwoDot, 2021.

Haralson, Danny. "Did You Know . . . What Fort Grant Dragged In with It, Part 2," *Eastern Arizona Courier*, June 19, 2016.

Jameson, W. C. *Billy the Kid: Investigating History's Mysteries*. Lanham, MD: TwoDot, 2018.

Lowe, Sam. *Jerks in New Mexico History*. Guilford, CT: Morris Book Publishing, 2012.

Michelson, Lynn. *Billy the Kid in Santa Fe*. Santa Fe, NM: Cleanan Press, 2019.

Moulton, Candy, trails historian. WWA Executive Director interview, February 2021.

Otero, Miguel Antonio. *The Real Billy the Kid with New Light on the Lincoln County War*. Santa Fe, NM: Sunstone Press, 2007.

Rasch, Philip J. *Trailing Billy the Kid*. Laramie, WY: National Association for Outlaw and Lawman History, Inc., 1995.

Silva, Jesus. *Amarillo Daily News*, November 13, 1936.

Simmons, Marc. *Stalking Billy the Kid: Brief Sketches of a Short Life*. Santa Fe, NM: Sunstone Press, 2006.

Simmons, Marc. "Trail Dust: Lew Wallace and Wife Found Early New Mexico Primitive." *The New Mexican*, March 15, 2013.

Thomas, David G. *The Trial of Billy the Kid*. Las Cruces, NM: Doc45 Publishing, 2021.

Tuska, Jon. *Billy the Kid: His Life and Legend*. Albuquerque: University of New Mexico Press, 1994.

Utley, Robert M. *Billy the Kid: A Short and Violent Life*. Lincoln: University of Nebraska Press, 1989.

Wallis, Michael. *Billy the Kid: The Endless Ride*. New York: Norton, 2007.

Weddle, Jerry. *Antrim Is My Stepfather's Name: The Childhood of Billy the Kid*. Tucson: Arizona Historical Society, 1993.

Wishart, David J., ed. *Encyclopedia of the Great Plains*. Lincoln: University of Nebraska Press, 2004. https://www.unl.edu/plains/pha/pha.shtml

Index

Italicized page numbers indicate photographs.

INDEX

ABOUT THE AUTHOR

New Mexico native **Melody Groves** loves anything western. Enchanted by the land where she grew up, she has explored ghost towns, ridden "steeds" across deserts, and lived in a pecan orchard. Winner of numerous honors, including the prestigious National Press Women Award, she writes fiction and nonfiction and for western magazines.

Melody lives life to the fullest. A world traveler, she also lived on Guam and later in the Philippines during the Vietnam War. The Southwest has always been in her heart, the Wild West especially. She has tried her hand at bull riding (eight seconds is a *long* time) and spent ten years as a gunfighter reenactor performing in Albuquerque's Old Town. She has battled good guys, bad guys, shrewy wives, and "dumb" husbands.

Her novels include *Border Ambush*, *Sonoran Rage*, *Arizona War*, *Kansas Bleeds*, *Black Range Revenge*, and *Trail to Tin Town*. She also authored *She Was Sheriff* and *Lady of the Law—The Maud Overstreet Saga*. Her nonfiction titles include *Ropes, Reins and Rawhide: All About Rodeo*, *Butterfield's Byways: America's Longest Mail Route across the West*, *Hoist a Cold One! Historic Bars of the Southwest*, and *When Outlaws Wore Badges*.

She lives in Albuquerque, New Mexico, and in her spare time plays rhythm guitar with the Jammy Time Band.